Demystifying Professional Learning Communities

School Leadership at Its Best

Edited by
Kristine Kiefer Hipp and Jane Bumpers Huffman

ROWMAN & LITTLEFIELD EDUCATION
A division of

ROWMAN & LITTLEFIELD PUBLISHERS, INC.
Lanham • New York • Toronto • Plymouth, UK

Published by Rowman & Littlefield Education
A division of Rowman & Littlefield Publishers, Inc.
A wholly owned subsidiary of The Rowman & Littlefield Publishing Group, Inc.
4501 Forbes Boulevard, Suite 200, Lanham, Maryland 20706
http://www.rowmaneducation.com

Estover Road, Plymouth PL6 7PY, United Kingdom

British Library Cataloguing in Publication Information Available

Library of Congress Cataloging-in-Publication Data

Demystifying professional learning communities : school leadership at its best / edited by Kristine Kiefer Hipp and Jane Bumpers Huffman.
    p. cm.
  Includes bibliographical references.
  ISBN 978-1-60709-049-6 (cloth : alk. paper) — ISBN 978-1-60709-050-2 (pbk. : alk. paper) — ISBN 978-1-60709-051-9 (electronic)
  1. Professional learning communities—United States. 2. Educational change—United States. I. Hipp, Kristine Kiefer, 1949- II. Huffman, Jane Bumpers, 1950-
  LB1731.D44 2010
  371.2'07—dc22   2009045705

∞ ™ The paper used in this publication meets the minimum requirements of American National Standard for Information Sciences—Permanence of Paper for Printed Library Materials, ANSI/NISO Z39.48-1992.
Printed in the United States of America

Kris Hipp dedicates this book to her mother and friend,
Evelyn Chartier Kiefer Sullivan and her late father,
Neil Timothy Sullivan.
Janie Huffman dedicates this book to her four grandchildren,
Chloe, Lilly, Charlotte, and Cole.
We would also like to dedicate our book to the educators who work so
hard to "get it right" by courageously and intentionally working to
create and sustain learning communities. We applaud your persistent
efforts and support your commitment to quality teaching and leading to
provide learning opportunities for all.

Contents

✛
Acknowledgments

We again want to recognize Shirley M. Hord, our friend and mentor, who has guided us since our work with Southwest Educational Development Laboratory. We also salute our research team, Anita M. Pankake, D'Ette Fly Cowan, Dianne F. Olivier, and Gayle Moller. We have worked together for 12 years and have grown to admire, respect, and enjoy each other as professionals and friends within our own professional learning community.

We would like to thank our other contributing authors, Linda Roundtree and Jesus Abrego, who provided additional information, experiences, and narrative for two of our chapters.

We are appreciative of our staff and colleagues at our universities and also want to thank our department chairs and deans for their support and encouragement.

Our heartfelt thanks goes to our editor, Leslie Blair, an amazing person who quickly and efficiently edited and formatted our book and prepared it for our publisher.

And, finally, we are very grateful for Maera Stratton and Tom Koerner of Rowman & Littlefield Education. Maera's patience and clear direction assisted us in keeping on schedule. Tom, who has advised us through both books, always provided wise council and a positive attitude. We appreciate both of you for having confidence in us as we worked our way to completion.

Foreword

Professionals learning together in community is a powerful concept! As most education professionals seek improvement for their schools, they realize that school improvement is based on change: changing programs, processes, and practices. They know that maintaining the status quo—continuing to do what they are currently doing—will produce the same results. Improvement means obtaining desired new results. Implementing change to achieve new results requires learning. This learning may focus on using new curriculum content, developing new instructional strategies, using data more effectively, or learning how to interact more effectively with students.

Professional educators agree that the purpose of schools is *student learning*. They also acknowledge that the most critical factor in whether students learn well is *quality teaching*. Quality teaching is increased or enhanced through *continuous professional learning* that targets the needs of students. The most productive context for the continuous learning of professionals is the *professional learning community* (PLC). Many schools believe they have established PLCs, but in reality they have not. Four essential questions assess the operation of the PLC.

WHAT ARE YOU LEARNING?

When school staff are invited to describe their PLC, many respond that their grade-level teams or academic departments hold meetings. Of course, this is an essential start, but only a start. What occurs in the meeting, though, seems fuzzy, unknown, or indescribable. Some teams report that they share expertise or what each person knows. Certainly, sharing experiences, materials, or successful activities with students can increase the members' repertoire. But is this learning what is needed by the teacher to address the needs of his or her students? Does the learning that the professional needs reside in the team members, or is it necessary to go outside the team or school to find the requisite learning?

Other respondents are likely to report the team's efforts to work collaboratively on various projects. Learning by the professionals may well occur as a by-product of working together. But is this accidental professional learning what is needed by the teacher to ensure specific student learning results? This is not often the case.

However, those involved with PLCs that are increasing staff learning and staff effectiveness report they have investigated numerous sources of student data to ascertain subject areas in which students are learning well and have identified those areas where student achievement is not so successful. Subsequently, the team reviews, reflects, and assesses their teaching quality in those areas of poor student gain. This exploration then provides the PLC with data-based indicators that direct their attention to *what* they need to retool, renew, or extend their expertise through learning new content, strategies, or approaches to address student needs.

WHY ARE YOU LEARNING THAT?

In a true PLC, staff learning is not casual. It is not the result of untargeted sharing of what each knows, and it does not depend on the PLC members' collective knowledge base to provide what is needed. It does not rely on the *possibility* that the members will learn what is needed through collaborative work together, no matter how fruitful that work may be in its products or processes.

The PLC members' learning is not only collegial—that is, they are learning in their community group—but it is *intentional*. The intentionality has been derived from the study of student data and defined in terms of what the professionals need to learn and change for students to learn more successfully. This study of the data suggests the following four steps:

1. Identification of desired new student learning results that address a change in the disappointing outcomes in the data that have been reviewed.
2. Specification of the knowledge and skills that team members need to achieve the desired new results for students.

3. Design and delivery of professional development (by the members themselves, by school or district professional development staff, or by others) that cultivates and nurtures the knowledge and skills specified for the professionals that enables them to achieve the new results for students.
4. Assessment of and access to system resources, policies, leadership, and culture that will support the three previous steps.

This schema makes clear that the learning of the professionals is directly related to the needs of students and the outcomes that have not been successfully met by students.

HOW ARE YOU LEARNING?

As noted, the professionals may be learning from each other through sharing their expertise—if it is targeted to the needs of students. It is possible, of course, to learn by working together, if the work provides opportunities for professional learning tied to student needs.

The PLC is a self-governing entity; therefore, the members have the option of deciding what to learn and how to learn and may draw on a broader context for their learning. For sure, they may seek learning from each other, but if what is to be learned does not reside in the community, then the PLC may seek colleagues on their campus for support and assistance. If this resource does not provide what is needed, then the PLC may look to colleagues in other schools or to district office staff for help in gaining their new knowledge and skills.

Many PLCs seek help and information through books and articles and engage collaboratively in book study that focuses on what the PLC determines it needs to learn. This use of book study must include not just the review of the text and its information, but also planning by the PLC about how staff will transfer the new knowledge back to their classroom for use with students. Oftentimes, this study is accompanied by specified plans that all agree to use to implement the new ideas and strategies in their teaching activities. This arms all staff members with a concrete plan that guides their introduction and installation of the new *way of doing* things. Application of the learning in their classrooms through a community-developed plan is followed by the group's review and reflection of how the plan worked and how it might need revision.

When it appears not possible to obtain particular learning at the home campus or district, then an expert may be engaged to bring specific expertise to the PLC, to satisfy their needs for learning that will increase their effectiveness. Again, follow-through is needed so that a one-day workshop with an expert or consultant becomes a successful way for the PLC to gain what is needed.

HOW ARE YOU DISSEMINATING YOUR LEARNING?

Lest the aforementioned ideas suggest that PLCs are organized only around grade levels in the elementary school or subject areas in the secondary school, the whole school also should be considered as a PLC. Meetings and learning in the small teams are important activities because they focus on the specific curriculum and student needs of that grade level or academic department.

But school data should be reviewed by the entire staff so that specific needs across the school may be addressed by the smaller groups, in addition to their specific grade or academic department demands. If the learning does not extend to the whole school, then a common purpose fails to be developed and supported across the campus. When this occurs, alignment of teaching and learning fails to materialize and students suffer from redundancies and gaps.

A system whereby all learning of the small groups and the whole campus group are shared should be designed. This can happen in a monthly (or more frequent) PLC meeting of the whole campus where all the parts report on their efforts, and where, in addition, whole group learning activities take place. Between whole campus meetings, sharing can occur in newsletters, electronically or on paper. Both the small team PLCs and the whole school PLC are needed, working in tandem or in a parallel fashion.

AND, SO?

As you can tell from the description just presented, becoming a true PLC is complex. How can you clarify your understanding of the PLC concept and make these ideas come alive in your school or district? This excellent volume by Hipp and Huffman gives you the answers and the suggestions to make it happen. This dynamic duo provides tools to enable the PLC to develop and to mature so that its learning and work are effective. Usefully, the book gives us an overview of the development of the PLC concept and how it is operationalized. Understanding how the PLC idea emanated helps us in gaining clarity about the PLC structure and the expectations for its work. Hipp and Huffman provide splendid examples of the dimensions of the PLC and what the PLC is and does. Without this clarity, so richly given to us by these two authors, there can be no progress toward developing a PLC in a school.

Importantly, tools that creators of PLCs may use in their schools are included in this volume. Significant instruments for assessing the presence and maturity of a PLC are also provided to the reader. Three different PLC school experiences come alive in richly detailed case stories that offer readers the opportunity to analyze and apply specific concepts and practices to their schools.

Hipp and Huffman, along with their contributing authors, add important information to the knowledge base on PLCs. They speak to both the novice and the experienced leader about the what, why, and how of PLCs. Communities of professional learners are arguably our best approach to improve the quality of teaching in our schools and the effectiveness of our schools' professionals in ensuring all students are successful learners.

Shirley M. Hord, Ph.D.
Senior Scholar Laureate
National Staff Development Council

1

Introduction

Jane Bumpers Huffman and Kristine Kiefer Hipp

With increased expectations for accountability in schools, concerns about administrator and teacher morale and retention, and the continuing challenge to address the needs of diverse and marginalized learners, the urgency of school reform calls school leaders to seek alternative ways to address these issues. New approaches come and go, but few result in significant school improvement that directly impact student learning. If researchers are accurate in maintaining that professional learning communities (PLCs) are the *best hope* for school reform, then school leaders must learn how to facilitate systemic processes to develop these instructional cultures (see Table 1.1). Specifically, leaders must assess their school context and student data, promote shared decision making across their school community, implement best practices by mobilizing immediate action, and hold themselves and others accountable for sustaining student success.

Nearly two decades ago, in *Restructuring America's Schools*, Lewis (1989) asserted that, "If schools are, as some charge, 'dismal places to work and learn,' it is because people have created them as such" (p. 220). Also, the challenges school communities face are exacerbated by the continual outbreaks of school violence and the increased numbers of school dropouts. School and community leaders and faculty in leadership preparation programs are addressing these and other critical issues. Clearly, we must all work and learn together to eliminate the apathy, mistrust, fear, and failure in schools, which pose a threat to our students, teachers, and administrators on a daily basis.

So, what issues and questions need to be addressed to meet these challenges?

- What are PLCs?
- How do PLCs look in schools and districts?
- What purposeful actions are useful in creating PLCs?
- How do you assess your staff and school in relation to the PLC concept?
- What strategies would you employ to achieve results?
- What are the benefits for staff and students?
- How do you continue to move schools forward and sustain your efforts toward student achievement?

This book offers information and examples to respond to these questions, to clarify the concept of a PLC, and to support educational leaders in addressing the important and critical mandates of accountability and school improvement. As school leaders proactively lead efforts to create PLCs, their school staff will incorporate knowledge, skills, and practices that focus on teaching and learning.

BACKGROUND

In contrast to the scientific management theory of organizing schools that dominated in the early part of the twentieth century, work during the same period by Dewey (1938) in progressive education led to the current constructivist ideologies that link learning with experience and context. This constructivist research is supported in the work of numerous researchers who laid much of the groundwork for current school reform (Fullan, 1993; Hord, 1997; McLaughlin, 1993; Newmann & Wehlage, 1995; Rosenholtz, 1989). These researchers proposed that PLCs, an approach to engaging school staffs in meaningful learning, can lead to increased student achievement.

In addition, during the 1980s, governmental and private sector leaders initiated efforts to address reform concerns. Response to the alarming 1983 National Commission on Excellence in Education report, *A Nation at Risk*, created a multitude of task forces collectively called "The Excellence Movement." This initiative offered an opportunity for educators to embark on serious reform of the educational system. No doubt the intentions were noble, and efforts were made to improve education for students; however, few new systemic initiatives or creative advances surfaced. Students and teachers were told to work harder and accomplish more with fewer resources. This bureaucratic top-down approach succeeded in alienating teachers and administrators, thus widening the gap between the decision making of policy makers and the real work in schools and classrooms.

The next two decades witnessed a proliferation of school reform initiatives to address student learning. The National Education Goals were set by the U.S. Congress in the 1990s to establish goals for standards-based education reform. Many of these goals addressed curriculum content, pupil performance, opportunity to learn, and assessment standards. This proclamation established a framework in which to identify world-class academic standards, to measure student progress, and to provide the support that students may need to meet the standards (Goals 2000: Educate America Act, 1994). Not all of the goals were attained by the year 2000, as was intended. The Goals 2000: Educate America Act is seen by many as the predecessor to No Child Left Behind 2001 (Public Law 107–110), which mandated measurable improvement in student achievement across all groups.

The No Child Left Behind Act of 2001, commonly known as NCLB, is a federal law that reauthorizes several federal programs that aim to improve the performance of America's pre-K–12 schools by increasing state, school district, and school accountability, as well as providing parents more flexibility in choosing which schools their students will attend.

The NCLB authorized federal programs targeting the improvement in the performance of elementary and secondary school students. In addition, standardized tests were mandated, and students would be expected to show improvement and be proficient by 2014. This act has been in effect since January 2002, has been reviewed numerous times, and has been a source of controversy and debate among educators at all levels. Debate is ongoing among legislators, policy makers, and educators, as the future of NCLB policies are called into question. The intent of NCLB and other school reforms continue with the anticipated reauthorization of the Elementary and Secondary Education Act (ESEA) and other federally directed priorities.

Although these government policies have influenced changes in many of our nation's schools, controversy surrounding the expectations and regulations required by these laws continues. As a result, the 10 federally funded regional education laboratories, private entities, including the Gates Foundation, the Wallace Foundation, the Broad Foundation, the Southern Regional Education Board (SREB), and others, have committed time, money, and additional resources to develop large-scale reform programs to also address school improvement issues.

Documentation of successful reform efforts provides evidence that some school efforts have resulted in increased student achievement. Yet, despite enthusiastic and substantial work by policy makers, educators, parents, and community members sustained advances in the majority of schools have yet to occur. In fact, serious problems remain, including violence and safety in schools; student discipline and dropout issues; lack of parent, community, and central office support; teacher and administrator retention and motivation; and poverty and class issues. These issues, unfortunately, continue to inhibit schools from being safe and successful nurturing learning environments for students and teachers. To address these issues, Fullan (2005) asserts that success depends on strategies that support leadership at all levels of the system and focuses on leaders who are able to develop other leaders. Working together they will interact and jointly lead change across the three levels of the system: school, district, and state.

THE CHALLENGE

Since Peter Senge published his landmark book, *The Fifth Discipline* (1990), and more recently, *Schools That Learn* (2000), leading educators continue to struggle with ways to initiate, implement, and sustain learning organizations, that is, cultures that provide hope for organizational reform. The struggle facing educators involves not only creating a clear vision for improvement and learning opportunities for educators and students, but also providing time for teachers and administrators to examine student data and to guide collaborative work and decisions.

Clearly, practitioners and researchers have provided organizations myriad images as to *how* these learning communities should look, but few school leaders have been successful in sustaining these communities over time. Ongoing research and reported pockets of success, as seen in the 2006 *Journal of School Leadership* special issue, "Leadership and Student Learning in Professional Learning Communities," leave us optimistic that schools organized around PLC practices that include action based on data analysis, positively affect student achievement. Although Senge (in Zemke, 1999) described the task of creating learning communities as formidable, "a slippery concept to put into practice" (p. 41), we remain hopeful and convinced that school leaders can, and must, create cultures that make a difference for students.

We are now challenged to expand on these pockets of success to determine innovative practices to improve schools by creating infrastructures that build individual, interpersonal, and organizational capacity. During the last decade, researchers have embraced the concept of PLCs and acknowledged the role that leadership plays as the foundation for essential systemic school reform (see Table 1.1).

Data reported in this book have been compiled from our longitudinal study from 1999 through 2007 regarding the development and documentation of our two study schools and related PLC practices. Thus, in our 12 years of research on PLCs we find teachers, administrators, paraprofes-

Table 1.1 Leadership, PLCs, and Systemic School Reform

Lambert, 1998 *Building Leadership* *Capacity in Schools*	Leadership is positioned as the central structure for creating PLCs through broad-based skillful participation; roles and responsibilities reflecting broad involvement and collaboration; and reflective practice and innovation.
Mitchell & Sackney, 2000 *Profound Improvement:* *Building Capacity for* *a Learning Community*	Infrastructures that involve work arrangements that bring people together to further the work of learning require transformative, empowering, facilitative, and decentralizing leadership. A learning community is a place where there are communities of leaders, where students, teachers, non-instructional staff, parents, and administrators share the opportunities and responsibilities for decision making.
Mulford & Silins, 2003 Leadership for Organisational Learning and Improved Student Outcomes—What Do We Know? *NSIN Research Matters*	Studied leadership that made a difference in a high school with a community focus, where staff felt valued, and organizational learning was transformational and distributed.
Fullan, 2002, 2005 *Leadership in a Culture of* *Change Professional Learning* *Communities Writ Large, On* *Common Ground*	Develop moral purpose for understanding change, direction, and results, building relationships, knowledge creation, and coherence building. Develop tri-level leadership to increase the capacity of the larger system to build and sustain PLCs.
Crowther, Kagan, **Ferguson & Hahn, 2002** *Developing Teacher Leaders:* *How Teacher Leadership* *Enhances School Success*	Parallel leadership is a process "that encourages a relatedness between teacher leaders and administrator leaders that activates and sustains the knowledge-generating capacity of schools" (p. 38), grounded in the values of mutual trust, shared directionality, and allowance for individual expression. This image assumes equivalence in leadership, where principals serve as strategic leaders and teachers assume responsibility for pedagogical leadership. Such school improvement processes link school-based leadership and improvement of student outcomes, reflective of the role learning communities play in school reform.
Huffman & Hipp, 2003 *Reculturing Schools as* *Professional Learning* *Communities*	"We maintain that future school leaders need to create communities of learners that include broad-based leadership built on shared visions that emerge from the relationships, values, beliefs, and commitments of the entire organization" (p. 146).

Hargreaves & Fink, 2006 *Sustainable Leadership*	Sustainable leadership reflects seven principles for sustainable educational change: depth, length, breadth, justice, diversity, resourcefulness, and conservation. Therefore, leadership (a) matters, (b) lasts, (c) spreads, (d) does no harm to and actively improves the surrounding environment, (e) promotes cohesive diversity, (f) develops and does not deplete material and human resources, and (g) honors and learns from the best of the past to create an even better future.
Journal of School Leadership, **Special Issue, 2006**, Leadership and Student Learning in Professional Learning Communities	This issue includes several articles that focus on the role of leadership in creating learning communities that advance student learning.
Moller & Pankake, 2006 *Lead with Me*	"Principals intentionally plan and facilitate the process of collaborative leadership. . . . Since teacher leaders will influence others one way or the other, we advocate that principals ensure that teacher leadership is focused on student learning" (p. 8).
Spillane, 2006 *Distributed Leadership*	School leadership requires both formal and informal leaders interacting and collaborating with a focus on learning. These actions direct and sustain PLCs.
DuFour, DuFour, & Eaker, 2008 *Revisiting Professional Learning Communities at Work*	"Principals . . . create the conditions that help the adults in their schools continually improve upon their collective capacity to ensure all students acquire the knowledge, skills, and dispositions essential to their success" (p. 310).
Hord & Sommers, 2008 *Leading Professional Learning Communities*	"The principal more than any other position in the school, identifies, models, and brings the policies and procedures to life. The principal's actions, not just his or her words, make believers out of teachers. And beyond the principal's actions, it takes the actions of the teacher leaders to create inclusive leadership" (p. 29).

sionals, and other instructional specialists serving in multiple leadership roles and working collaboratively to establish learning cultures that support student achievement. A preliminary study (1995–2000) directed by Shirley Hord at the Southwest Educational Development Laboratory (SEDL) laid the foundation for our research.

PURPOSE OF BOOK

The purpose of this book is to clearly define an approach to school improvement that uses PLC practices to achieve success for every student. Chapters 1–3 introduce and demystify the PLC concept, offer supporting literature related to PLCs, and examine the development of our methodology and conceptual framework. Chapters 4–6 present formal and informal assessment tools, processes, and a teaching and learning cycle that advances professional dialogue about the effectiveness of classroom practices using student work as data.

Chapters 7–10 introduce and include three case stories that provide educators opportunities to review and explore real-life examples of intentional efforts to create and sustain PLCs. Chapters 11–12 address the challenges of sustainability and leading complex adaptive change in schools and districts. We hope our findings assist leaders, change agents, policy makers, and university faculty in guiding schools toward creating and maintaining PLCs as they sustain school improvement for adults and student learning.

ORGANIZATION OF THE BOOK

In this book, we build on the information presented in our first book, *Reculturing Schools as Professional Learning Communities* (Huffman & Hipp, 2003) and reveal rich data we continue to collect. We hope our readers use this information in elementary and secondary schools, in leadership preparation courses and venues, and in policy arenas to develop strong instructional and cultural strategies for increased student achievement. Specifically, our book provides the following:

- Chapter 1, Introduction, presents challenges, issues, and questions to meet these challenges, a brief background related to school reform efforts, literature that reveals the impact of leadership, PLCs and systemic school reform, and the purpose and organization of the book.
- Chapter 2, Demystifying the Concept of Professional Learning Communities, is a historical account of the research related to PLCs and what we have learned from the literature.
- Chapter 3, Methodology and Conceptual Framework, shares the data collection, data analysis, and documentation of Phase 4 of our research. This chapter also provides a conceptual organizer that offers a visual depiction of the PLC model incorporating Critical Attributes and Phases of Change.

- Chapter 4, Assessing and Analyzing Schools as Professional Learning Communities, presents a formal assessment tool to analyze schools as PLCs and a scale to measure teachers' collective efficacy. We also share examples of and relationships between collective efficacy and leadership capacity evident in mature PLCs. Finally, dialogue skills are presented to guide teachers and administrators in processing information and taking action related to data analysis.
- Chapter 5, Diagnostic and Planning Tools, presents several informal diagnostic tools. In addition we include an initial planning form to assist leaders in getting started.
- Chapter 6, The Professional Teaching and Learning Cycle: A Strategy for Creating Professional Learning Communities provides a teaching and learning process that systemically aligns curriculum, instruction, and assessment to state standards. A guiding vignette is offered to assist teachers to implement the process.
- Chapter 7, Case Story Overview, presents an overview of the case story format. It also addresses issues around collective efficacy, leadership capacity, and external factors. This provides an opportunity for educators to review and explore practices in exemplary PLCs, address issues of three case study schools, ponder critical questions, and develop plans to apply learning in home schools.
- Chapter 8, Case Story #1: Lake Elementary (PreK–8), details how administrators and teacher leaders work collaboratively toward sustaining a PLC.
- Chapter 9, Case Story #2: Mineral Springs Middle School (6–8), describes how school faculty and staff struggle through leadership changes to continue implementing PLC efforts.
- Chapter 10, Case Story #3: Ralph H. Metcalfe School (K4–8), reveals how an incoming principal begins to reculture a school to initiate PLC efforts.
- Chapter 11, Sustainability: A Constant Process for Continuing Improvement, utilizes a metaphorical approach to scenarios, suggestions, and strategies that make sustainability achievable.
- Chapter 12, Final Reflections: Moving Schools Forward, includes reflections, concluding insights, and remaining challenges that educators today face in sustaining school improvement efforts to impact learning for all students.

Our research is supported and inspired by collaborative research teams in Australia, Canada, the United Kingdom, as well as the United States. Our current efforts address critical issues in schools at all levels and in multiple contexts including rural, urban, and suburban schools. Building on this knowledge, we are convinced that PLCs can be created and sustained to address urgent issues that confront schools in the United States including: leadership succession, collective efficacy, urban issues of race and class, high school reform, leadership capacity, and technical and adaptive change. Although these challenges appear daunting, we support Schmoker's (2006) belief that:

> Professional learning communities have emerged as arguably the best, most agreed upon means to continuously improve instruction and student performance. For reasons that will become clear, they succeed where typical staff development and workshops fail. (p. 106)

2

✛

Demystifying the Concept of Professional Learning Communities

Kristine Kiefer Hipp and Jane Bumpers Huffman

The challenge for school leadership this millennium is to guide their school communities from concept to capability—a capability that is self-sustaining and that will institutionalize reform—A New Approach.

—Huffman & Hipp, 2003, p. 149

WHY DEVELOP PROFESSIONAL LEARNING COMMUNITIES?

Steven Covey's (2004) advice to *begin with the end in mind* reminds us of the importance of beginning with a clear vision of what we are striving to achieve. Accordingly, the purpose of this chapter is to provide the reader with a clear sense of what PLCs are and how schools that have evolved into such organizations operate.

The term *professional learning community* actually emerged from organizational theory and human relations literature. As early as 1990, Peter Senge defined a learning organization, through a corporate perspective, as one in which "people continually expand their capacity to create desired results, where new and expansive patterns of thinking are nurtured, where collective aspiration is set free" (p. 3).

When applied to an educational setting, researchers define the concept as a school's professional staff who continuously seek to find answers through inquiry and then act on their learning to improve student learning. Shirley Hord (1997), an internationally known pioneer in the field of school improvement, defines a PLC as the professional staff learning together to direct efforts toward improved student learning.

11

In a more current publication, *Leading Professional Learning Communities,* Hord and Sommers (2008) emphasize the work of PLCs as "continuous and intentional staff learning, so that staff always are increasing their effectiveness leading to students' increased successful learning" (p. 24). Put simply, "The bottom line of the PLC is staff learning in order to increase student learning" (p. 20).

The value of PLCs in improving student learning is widely accepted in the educational community (Hord, 1997, 2004; Hord & Sommers, 2008; Louis & Kruse, 1995; Newmann & Wehlage, 1995; Olivier & Hipp, 2006; Rosenholtz, 1989; Sackney, Mitchell, & Walker, 2005; Schmoker, 2006). Currently, researchers and practitioners maintain that the concept of a PLC is perceived as *the promise* for school change and lasting reform.

Lieberman and Miller (1999) described PLCs as "places in which teachers pursue clear, shared purposes for student learning, engage in collaborative activities to achieve their purposes, and take collective responsibility for student learning" (p. 53). Moreover, Protheroe (2004) described a PLC as a school having "a culture that recognizes and capitalizes on the collective strengths and talents of its staff" (p. 1).

We believe the connection between culture and learning organizations is critical. We recognize that dynamic school cultures contribute to creating PLCs through norms, values, and relationships that sustain momentum for school improvement over time.

The notion of PLCs must be understood clearly for educators to regard the PLC model as a viable and lasting option for school reform. "The challenge for school leaders in this millennium is to guide their school communities from concept to capability—a capability that is self-sustaining and that will institutionalize reform—*A New Approach*" (Huffman & Hipp, 2003, p. 149).

Due to marginal implementation of initial change efforts and the instability often found in urban schools, Hipp and Weber (2008) further explain, "Creating PLCs in schools is difficult, but sustaining them is even more challenging, particularly in complex urban school districts" (p. 46).

Again, our intent is to demystify the concept of a PLC. Therefore, our definition explains the focus of our work as related to sustaining teacher and student learning: *Professional educators working collectively and purposefully to create and sustain a culture of learning for all students and adults.* To further demystify PLCs we will define and describe five dimensions that serve as the foundation of our work.

DEFINING THE DIMENSIONS OF
A PROFESSIONAL LEARNING COMMUNITY

After an extensive review of the literature surrounding PLCs, combined with field-based research, common practices emerged including:

- shared leadership,
- continuous inquiry and learning,
- shared practice,
- creation of collaborative structures and relationships, and, most importantly,
- an undeviating focus on student learning as the ultimate desired outcome (Hord, 1997).

These descriptions help us to visualize the culture and practices desired in a school and as Covey suggests begin with *the end in mind*. Developing, nurturing, and sustaining a community of learners is no small endeavor and requires intentional actions on the part of formal leaders. Taken together, the five dimensions developed by Hord provide a holistic picture of how a PLC operates, as well as actions leaders need to take to create such a culture. As a result of our research, we have modified these dimensions as follows:

1. Supportive and shared leadership: School administrators share power, authority, and decision making, while promoting and nurturing leadership.
2. Shared values and vision: The staff share visions that have an undeviating focus on student learning and support norms of behavior that guide decisions about teaching and learning.
3. Collective learning and application: The staff share information and work collaboratively to plan, solve problems, and improve learning opportunities.
4. Shared personal practice: Peers meet and observe one another to provide feedback on instructional practices, to assist in student learning, and to increase human capacity.
5. Supportive conditions: Relationships include respect, trust, norms of critical inquiry and improvement, and positive, caring relationships among the entire school community. Structures include systems (i.e., communication and technology) and resources (i.e., personnel, facilities, time, fiscal, and materials) to enable staff to meet and examine practices and student outcomes.

In the next sections, we offer insights gained from our research, and fieldwork. Moreover, we provide literature that aligns with our perception of the PLC concept.

Shared and Supportive Leadership

> "Ultimately, your leadership in a culture of change will be judged as effective or ineffective, not by who you are as a leader but by *what leadership you produce in others.*"
>
> —Michael Fullan, 2002, p. 137

Hord (1997) explains that supportive and shared leadership is evident when school administrators share power, authority, and decision making with teachers.

In mature PLCs the role of the principal was significant. Principals adept at building leadership capacity and achieving school goals disperse power, gather input into decisions, and encourage staff to focus on a common vision and mission.

Eaker, DuFour, and Burnette (2002) note that a fundamental cultural shift occurs when schools become PLCs, particularly in the way teacher leadership is nurtured. They state that "in traditional schools, administrators are viewed as being in leadership positions, while teachers are viewed as 'implementers' or followers. In professional learning communities, administrators are viewed as leaders of leaders" (p. 22).

Similarly, Marzano (2003) states that one of the common misconceptions about leadership at the school level is that it should reside with a single individual, in most cases, the principal. In *What Works in Schools,* he observes that "although it is certainly true that strong leadership from the principal can be a powerful force toward school reform, the notion that an individual effects change by sheer will and personality is simply not supported by the research" (p. 174).

Lambert (1998a), in *Building Leadership Capacity in Schools,* supports this concept in her assertion that,

> School leadership needs to be a broad concept that is separated from person, role, and a discreet set of individual behaviors. It needs to be embedded in the school community as a whole. Such a broadening of the concept of leadership suggests shared responsibility for a shared purpose of community. (p. 5)

In a special issue devoted to teacher leadership in *Leading and Managing, a Journal of the Australian Council of Educational Leaders,* Hipp's (2004) research reinforces the significance of this concept, "when leadership was shared, principals were not viewed as abdicating their responsibility, but as purposefully building capacity . . . Administrators view[ed] as themselves as facilitators of learning and help[ed] with teaching to collectively meet the needs of students" (p. 65).

Together, committed leadership provided by teachers and administrators establishes a school culture that supports student learning. Moreover, Hipp and her colleagues found that teacher professional commitment was the "key variable in developing and sustaining a rich professional culture" (Olivier, Pankake, Hipp, Cowan, & Huffman, 2005, p. 35). Clearly, teachers play a critical role in establishing an environment that assumes responsibility for all students' success.

This new view of leadership in which administrators and teachers assume shared responsibility for decision making requires intentional action on the part of formal leaders. In her landmark book, *Leading to Change*, Johnson (1996) emphasizes:

> Today's school leaders must understand both the limits and the potential of their positions, carefully balancing their use of positional authority with their reliance on others, gradually building both a capacity and widespread support for shared leadership and collaborative change. (p. 11)

Similarly, Fullan (2002) asserts, "The role of leadership is to 'cause' greater capacity in the organization in order to get better results" (p. 65). Shared leadership fosters a multitude of interactions and relationships that build capacity for change, particularly because these changes promote increased student learning.

Glickman (2002) suggests that if a school leader understands that the "use of multiple structures with multiple leaders for assisting, focusing, and improving classroom teaching and learning, then continuous improvement can become an ongoing reality" (p. 9). And Rost, more specifically proposes, "Leadership is an influence relationship among leaders and collaborators who intend significant changes that reflect their mutual purposes" (personal communication, June 20, 2007).

Moller and Pankake (2006) contend that this new leadership structure emerges within a community of learners "focused on the moral purpose of schooling—improved student learning" (p. 6). Shared and supportive leadership to pursue this purpose emerges as a critical dimension of a PLC.

Shared Values and Vision

"Among the key features of a school community is a core of shared values about what students should learn, about how faculty and students should behave, and about the shared aims to maintain community."

—Karen Louis and Sharon Kruse, 1995, p. 16

An effective vision presents a credible yet realistic picture of the organization that inspires the participants to work toward a future goal. According to Hord (1997), the concept of a learning community embraces shared values and vision that "lead to binding norms of behavior that the staff support" (p. 3).

This vision for school improvement emerges when it is characterized by an undeviating focus on student learning. Huffman and Hipp (2003) report, "Ideally, shared values would inspire a shared vision among diverse stakeholders, and student focused decisions would be connected to site goals" (p. 145).

Olivier, Cowan, and Pankake (2000) further pose that although "schools pay attention to many things, matters that make a difference are at times neglected, such as how schools operate to enhance student learning. The development of shared values can serve to help staff identify what is vitally important" (p. 145).

It has become apparent that if those within schools lack a common vision, it is highly unlikely they will achieve desired outcomes. Senge (1990) states this quite emphatically as it relates to its importance in a PLC: "You cannot have a learning organization without a shared vision" (p. 209).

Similarly, DuFour and Eaker (1998) note that "the lack of a compelling vision for public schools continues to be a major obstacle in any effort to improve schools" (p. 64) and emphasize that a crucial component for a successful PLC is a foundation that includes mission, vision, values, and goals collaboratively developed.

Collaborative vision building is the initial challenge for learning communities. Simply declaring a vision by a school leader and imposing it on the organization will not generate the collective energy needed to propel an organization forward.

Barth (1990) suggests that, "Honoring the visions of others, maintaining fidelity to one's own vision, and at the same time working toward a collective vision and coherent institutional purpose constitute an extraordinary definition of school leadership and represent one of the most important undertakings facing those who would improve schools from within" (p. 156).

The central task of a leader, therefore, is to involve others in creating a shared vision for the organization that connects teaching and learning and developing a PLC. Personal visions must be developed and integrated with others so that a collective vision can be modeled and embraced by all members. Furthermore, this vision must be sufficiently compelling to pull everyone toward its realization (Moller & Pankake, 2006).

Collective Learning and Application

"The most successful schools . . . created opportunities for teachers to collaborate and help one another achieve the purpose; and teachers in these schools took collective—not just individual—responsibility for student learning."

(Neumann & Wehlage, 1995, p. 3)

A key to building community within a school involves dedication to the process of inquiry and learning; this then, becomes the basis for decisions in schools and classrooms. Sergiovanni (1994) contends that the very act of learning together exerts a powerful influence on the sense of community in a school, "As we learn together and as we inquire together, we create the ties that enable us to become a learning community" (p. 167).

Hord (1997) notes that PLCs promote continuous learning by all staff on matters central to a school's primary improvement initiatives and promote high intellectual tasks and solutions to address student needs.

Learning takes many forms, ranging from traditional professional development practices, such as participation in workshops, to job-embedded learning that emphasizes "learning by doing, reflecting on the experience, and then generating and sharing new insights and learning with oneself and others" (Wood & McQuarrie, 1999, p. 10). In the latter form, professional development becomes an ongoing activity in the various educational processes of operating schools including curriculum development, student assessment, and the development and evaluation of instructional strategies. Because it is embedded, professional development becomes an indispensable dimension of a PLC.

When teachers learn together, by engaging in open dialogue, opportunities arise to collaborate and apply new knowledge, skills, and strategies. Moreover, day-to-day practices within PLCs foster the role of teachers as learners.

In *Sustaining Professional Learning Communities*, Blankstein, Houston, and Cole (2007) offer multiple overlapping steps that guide staff efforts. These steps begin with assessing the impact of teachers' current work on student outcomes and using data to identify priorities and ending with review and revision.

In observing mature PLCs, they "recognize that student learning [is] a function of teacher learning. In other words, teachers [see] themselves as the *first learners*" (Olivier et al., 2005, p. 35). As teachers apply what they have learned, reflect on the process, and in turn, discuss the results of their practices, doors open to continuous learning through shared personal practice.

Shared Personal Practice

> "What might we [teachers] do to the work we provide students to make it more engaging and compelling? . . . Teachers, like other leaders, should be evaluated and assessed on the basis of what they get others to do, not on what they do themselves."
>
> —Phillip C. Schlechty, 1997, pp. 181, 185

As teachers interact, we find shared personal practice involves observing and providing feedback and sharing new practices in both formal and informal settings. Yet, Hipp and Weber (2008) reveal that this essential element in becoming a PLC is least evident in most schools.

To achieve conditions that support shared personal practice, Midgley and Wood (1993) contend that "teachers need an environment that values and supports hard work, the acceptance of challenging tasks, risk taking, and the promotion of growth" (p. 252). An environment that values such endeavors is enhanced by processes that encourage teachers to share their personal practices with one another.

According to Hord (1997), this PLC dimension necessitates peer review and feedback on instructional practice to increase individual and organizational capacity. Louis and Kruse (1995) called this *deprivatization of practice* and maintained that review of a teacher's instructional practice by colleagues is the norm in the PLC. This review is not an evaluative procedure but serves as a part of the *peers helping peers* process.

One example of this practice is for teachers to exchange student work samples with colleagues to be reviewed as evidence of effective instructional practice. Another example is for teachers to visit their colleagues' classrooms to observe, take notes, and discuss their observations (Bushman, 2006). Teachers participate in debate, discussion, and disagreement; they share their successes and their failures (Bushman, 2006; Protheroe, 2004).

Within PLCs, these types of activities are transparent, highly valued, and occur on a regular, ongoing basis with a structured process to guide interactions. In these cultures, teachers are always collectively committed to the work of increasing student learning.

Supportive Conditions

> "Current conditions in the schools—the isolation, the difficulty in assessing one's effectiveness as a teacher, the lack of collegial and administrative support, and the sense of powerlessness that comes from limited collegial decision-making make it difficult for teachers to maintain a strong sense of efficacy."
>
> —Patricia Ashton, 1984, p. 28

Supporting the work of learning communities requires leaders to address supportive conditions. Hord (1997) defined this dimension as school conditions and capacities that support the staff's arrangement as a professional learning organization.

Throughout our work, we found supportive conditions to be the glue that holds all other dimensions together. Writers and researchers (Boyd, 1992; DuFour & Eaker, 1998; Hord, 1997; Huffman & Hipp, 2003; Louis & Kruse, 1995; LaFee, 2003; Protheroe, 2004) noted two types of conditions as necessary to build effective learning communities: structural conditions and relationships. These factors support the work of teachers and administrators by providing time and opportunities to communicate regularly, plan collectively, problem solve, and learn.

Structures

Schools that are operating as PLCs must foster a culture in which learning by all is valued, encouraged, and supported, and in which, "the staff, intentionally and collectively, engage in learning and work on issues directly related to classroom practice that positively impacts student learning" (Cowan & Hord, 1999, p. 4). In practice, structures such as time and proximity are often provided by administrators and allow staff members to come together to work and learn.

Structures come in several shapes and sizes. Several researchers (Hollins, 2006; Louis & Kruse, 1995; Protheroe, 2004; Wiggins & McTighe, 2006) identify physical conditions needed to support communities of learners. They may include

- time to meet and dialogue,
- physical proximity of the staff to one another in departments or grade-level groups,
- small school size,
- collaborative teaching roles and responsibilities,
- effective communication programs,
- autonomous school units that are connected in meaningful ways to the district office and personnel, and
- intentional arrangements for teachers to influence decision making.

Time for teachers to work together is essential for school reform initiatives. Common planning time within the regular workday provides teachers the professional time necessary for collaborative work without impinging on their personal time.

The need to make time for such activities was emphasized in a proliferation of national reports on the use of time in schools during the middle

1990s (National Education Association Special Committee on Time Resources, 1993; National Educational Commission on Time and Learning, 1994; Purnell & Hill, 1992). These reports stressed that time in the school day must be restructured to provide educators an opportunity to make meaning of new changes demanded of them.

Many districts are addressing the issues around time. For instance, in *School Scheduling Strategies: New Ways of Finding Time for Students and Staff* (2003), Schroth, Beaty, and Dunbar propose several strategies for embedding time in the school day for staff development, planning, and meetings. Administrators throughout the nation are working with their communities to buy time during the school day in the form of early releases, late starts, banking time, block scheduling, reorganizing time within the day, team teaching, and small learning communities.

These structural conditions are clearly important so staff and administration have available resources to conduct their work without major logistical barriers. However, Schlechty (1997) points out that "structural change that is not supported by cultural change will eventually be overwhelmed by the culture, for it is in the culture that any organization finds meaning and stability" (p. 136).

Relationships

Boyd (1992) describes the people or cultural factors that create a meaningful and stable culture. Such factors include teacher attitudes that are consistently positive; norms that support ongoing learning and improvement, not the status quo; teachers who share and learn with each other; and a sense of responsibility for student learning and success.

Underlying such a culture is an emphasis on both individual and whole school improvement, which is rendered possible only after mutual respect and trustworthiness have been established among staff members.

"Without creating a culture of trust, respect, and inclusiveness with a focus on relationships, even the most innovative means of finding time, resources and developing communication systems will have little effect on creating a community of learners" (Huffman & Hipp, 2003, p. 146).

Tschannen-Moran (2004) asserts that due to the hierarchical nature of relationships in schools, it is the responsibility of the person in the position of most power to build and sustain trusting relationships. She maintains that trust matters because the quality of interpersonal relationships between adults in the school setting influences not only the climate and morale, but also makes a difference with student achievement.

Finally, Wignall (1992) describes a high school in which teachers share their practice and enjoy high levels of collaboration in their daily work life. He notes that mutual respect and understanding are fundamental requirements of such a workplace culture. This culture fosters an environment in which teachers find help, support, and trust among their colleagues as a result of the development of warm, professional relationships.

In schools in which strong relationships exist, there is also recognition of the achievements by staff members at faculty meetings and on other occasions. Celebrations of important events and outstanding successes occur and serve to create a reinforcing culture in which people look forward to coming to school each day. As well, these cultures are characterized by the understanding that risk-taking and experimenting with new approaches are acceptable and even encouraged. The environment is safe—physically, mentally, and emotionally.

SUMMARY

In our attempt to demystify the concept of a PLC, we identified literature and practices that are aligned with our model. Over the course of our work, we have witnessed a variety of perceptions in defining and describing the PLC concept.

It seems that the term *professional learning community* is often used to describe small groups, such as committees and departments, as well as large groups and entire schools, including all stakeholders (i.e., teachers, students, staff, school and district-level administrators, parents, and community members). The lack of a consistently used, common definition for PLCs only serves to confuse the practitioner.

To clarify our beliefs, we continue to report our research, fieldwork, and observations. As a result, we believe that reculturing schools as PLCs includes the following: (a) a whole school focus, (b) efforts based on the five PLC dimensions, and (c) participation by all professional staff in the school.

We also recognize the importance of additional stakeholders, such as central office personnel, parents, and community members, as support systems for the professional staff in their PLC efforts.

We contend PLCs require creativity and thoughtful and coordinated planning, implementation, and maintenance to continually advance student achievement.

The following chapters clarify *how* PLCs are formed and sustained. Specifically, Chapter 3 offers information regarding the methods used to gather and analyze data during five phases of research. The description of longitudinal research explains how our work with PLCs began and provides the framework for presenting findings from our research. This information brings greater detail to the big picture of *how* schools engage in creating and sustaining PLCs.

3

Methodology and Conceptual Framework

Jane Bumpers Huffman and Kristine Kiefer Hipp

In 1995, Fullan predicted, "change will require a radical reculturing of the school as an institution, and the basic redesign of the teaching profession" (p. 230). Such redesign occurs by developing values, norms, and attitudes that affect the core of the culture of schools, which necessitates change. To implement and sustain change there is also a need to develop leadership capacity, collective efficacy, collaborative learning, and more accountability across the entire school community.

The first section in this chapter reveals the methodology of our study documenting practices in high performing schools that have shown progress toward sustaining their current organizations as PLCs. The next section familiarizes the reader with a three-phase model describing the process of change. Finally, an organizer is presented depicting school practices at levels of initiation through implementation to sustainability.

METHODOLOGY

The research that undergirds the findings in this book is one component of a multi-method, 5-year study (1995–2000) of the development of PLCs—schools that continuously inquire and seek to improve teaching and learning (see Table 3.1). This first study was conducted by SEDL, funded under a contract with the U.S. Department of Education, and led by Shirley Hord.

Since the initial study, our research team conducted ongoing research in the two highest performing schools that emerged from the original study since 2001 (see Table 3.2).

Table 3.1   Initial 5-Year Professional Learning Community Project Schedule, 1995–2000

1995–1996: Phase 1	• Review of the literature
1996–1997	• Search for PLC schools
1997–1998: Phase 2	• Training of co-developers • Selection of study sites • *School Professional Staff as Learning Community Questionnaire*
1998–1999	• Continuous training of co-developers • Initial phone interviews with school principals and teacher representatives • *School Professional Staff as Learning Community Questionnaire*
1999–2000: Phase 3	• Continuous training of co-developers • Follow-up interviews with school principals and teacher representatives • On-site interviews of teaching staff in study schools conducted by SEDL staff and co-developer • *School Professional Staff as Learning Community Questionnaire*

Table 3.2   Research Schedule, 2001–2007

2001–2004: Phase 4	• On-site interviews, *Professional Learning Community Assessment* (PLCA), *Teacher Efficacy Beliefs Scale-Collective Form* (TEBS-C), *Leadership Capacity School Survey* (LCSS), document review, and informal observations
2005–2007: Phase 5	• On-site interviews, central office interviews, *Professional Learning Community Assessment* (PLCA), document review, and informal observations

Researchers analyzed interviews using a variety of related indicators to examine and substantiate the thoroughness of Hord's (1997) model of the five dimensions that constitute a PLC. Using qualitative analysis methods, we identified critical attributes of each dimension. Although the dimensions are discussed as separate and discreet, we analyzed them holistically due to the overlapping characteristics found within the dimensions. The critical attributes of each dimension are listed below (see also Figure 3.1).

Shared and Supportive Leadership

- Nurturing leadership among staff.
- Shared power, authority, and responsibility.
- Broad-based decision making that reflects commitment and accountability.
- Sharing information.

Shared Values and Vision

- Espoused values and norms.
- Focus on student learning.
- High expectations.
- Shared vision guides teaching and learning.

Collective Learning and Application

- Sharing information.
- Seeking new knowledge, skills, and strategies.
- Working collaboratively to plan, solve problems, and improve learning opportunities.

Shared Personal Practice

- Peer observations to offer knowledge, skills, and encouragement.
- Feedback to improve instructional practices.
- Sharing outcomes of instructional practices.
- Coaching and mentoring.

Supportive Conditions
Structures

- Resources (time, money, materials, people).
- Facilities.
- Communication systems.

Relationships

- Caring relationships.
- Trust and respect.
- Recognition and celebration.
- Risk-taking.
- Unified effort to embed change.

PHASES OF CHANGE TO INCREASE LEARNING

The success of schools functioning as PLCs that impact student and adult learning is dependent on how well staff members can sustain their efforts and embed effective practices into the culture of their school. If new practices are viewed as short-term or quick fixes to perceived problems, the impact will be superficial, confined to a few participants, and generally ineffective. Thus, we explored the question: *How do schools maintain momentum and long-term success in the change process?*

Central to the success of any substantive change is an understanding of how such change processes are defined and managed. Initially we utilized Fullan's (1990) three phases of change: initiation, implementation, and institutionalization, including 14 success factors (see Table 3.3).

Schools in the *initiation phase* generally connect a change initiative to student needs based on the school's values and norms. A strong leader promotes a shared vision and staff begin to dialogue, share information, seek new knowledge, and commit to the effort to achieve their goals.

During the *implementation phase,* a leader encourages the staff to set high expectations and enables them to meet their goals by sharing power, authority, and responsibility. Feedback and support related to instruction are evident, which leads to increased student outcomes. Nonetheless, progress is not always smooth.

The initiative being implemented often mirrors Fullan's *Implementation Dip,* reflecting that initiation of change is often accompanied by a series of

Table 3.3 Phases of Change

Initiation	Implementation	Institutionalization
Linked to high profile needs	Orchestration Shared control	Embedding Linked to instruction
A clear model	Pressure and support	Widespread use
Strong advocate	Technical assistance	Removal of competing priorities
Active initiation	Rewards	Continuing assistance

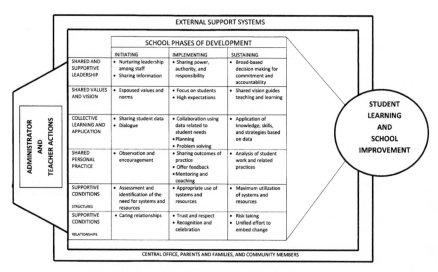

Figure 3.1. Professional Learning Community Organizer (PLCO)

setbacks that hinder progress. These setbacks can be due to a lack of resources and technical assistance and cause frustration, anxiety, and a sense of hopelessness.

Staffs that prevail through these uncertain times usually move to the *institutionalization phase,* in which the change initiative becomes embedded into the culture of the school. Guided by a shared vision, the school community is committed and accountable for student learning. They identify and solve problems amid a climate that invites risk-taking and therefore continual refocusing.

Institutionalization is the phase of change that is seldom addressed by the vast majority of schools in their improvement efforts. This omission is reported in our research as well. Our belief is that institutionalization across the five PLC dimensions is essential for schools to engage in sustained improvement and for continuous learning to occur.

PROFESSIONAL LEARNING COMMUNITY ORGANIZER CONCEPTUALIZATION AND DEVELOPMENT

As we studied schools in Phase 4, we conceptualized Hord's five dimensions in a new light, as illustrated in the Professional Learning Community Organizer (PLCO). See Figure 3.1.

First, we saw a critical link between *collective learning and application* and *shared personal practice.* We believe that these elements could not be separated and, therefore, should be placed together in this *non-sequential* set of dimensions.

Second, we viewed *supportive conditions* encompassing the other four dimensions, similar to the way Peter Senge (1990) views the discipline of *systems thinking,* the fifth discipline. We contend that without a strong culture of trust and respect, and related structures that promote continual learning, it is impossible to build a PLC.

Third, as critical attributes emerged throughout these interviews, they logically fell on a continuum reflecting evidence at the levels of initiation, implementation, and institutionalization. From our experience, which is supported by research (Fullan, 2005; Hipp, Huffman, Pankake, & Olivier, 2008; Stoll, McMahon, & Thomas, 2006), institutionalization is more accurately represented by the term *sustainability.* Thus, we modified Fullan's Phases of Change to reflect the importance of sustaining change.

Our reconceptualization reflects a more fluid process that emphasizes continuous improvement. Fullan (2005) recognized sustainability as related to the system's capacity to engage in continuous improvement based on values.

Next, Chapters 4 and 5 present formal and informal assessment tools, and processes including dialogue, developmental rubrics, and a PLC planning template. In addition, Chapter 6 provides a teaching and learning cycle that assists leaders in advancing professional dialogue about the effectiveness of classroom practices based on student work as data.

4

Assessing and Analyzing Schools as Professional Learning Communities

Dianne F. Olivier and Kristine Kiefer Hipp

If educators are indeed persuaded that transforming schools into PLCs offers the best strategy for school improvement, they must first establish a clear vision of what a learning community looks like and how people operate in such an organization. This vision can be enhanced by examining critical attributes of each dimension of a PLC, as listed in Chapter 3. Looking at the dimensions at the attribute level can also provide a more comprehensive description and understanding of the impact of the learning community on both teacher and student learning.

Although many educators believe their school operates as a learning community, closer investigation often reveals that they rarely meets the true operational criteria. Schools that function as PLCs have an underlying culture that values and supports learning by all, as well as honest and forthright dialogue about the effectiveness of their instructional practices. Cowan and Hord (1999) note that within such communities, "the staff, intentionally and collectively, engage in learning and work on issues directly related to classroom practice that positively impacts student learning" (p. 4).

Identifying schools that actually operate as PLCs offers a challenge for researchers, principals, staff, parents, and other stakeholders. Rather than determining that a school is or is not functioning as a PLC, it is more useful to assess its progress along a continuum by analyzing specific school and classroom practices. Such analysis can be enhanced by assessment of organizational variables related to PLC development, such as collective efficacy and leadership capacity.

Our conceptualization of the PLC dimensions and related attributes and the development of the PLCO introduced in Chapter 3 led to the development of a formal diagnostic tool to help educators determine where their school lies along a continuum. This instrument helps align staff perceptions and day-to-day actions and more accurately represent phases of PLC development: initiating (starting), implementing (doing), and institutionalizing (sustaining).

PROFESSIONAL LEARNING COMMUNITY ASSESSMENT—REVISED

The *Professional Learning Community Assessment* (PLCA) was initially created to assess everyday classroom and school-level practices in relation to PLC dimensions (Olivier, Hipp, & Huffman, 2003). The measure has been administered to professional staff in numerous school districts at varying grade levels throughout the United States. This assessment has assisted educators and researchers in determining the strength of practices in their own schools within each dimension.

The widespread use of the instrument provided an opportunity to review the dimensions for internal consistency. Our most recent analyses of this diagnostic tool has confirmed internal consistency resulting in the following Cronbach Alpha reliability coefficients for factored subscales (n=1209): Shared and Supportive Leadership (.94); Shared Values and Vision (.92); Collective Learning and Application (.91); Shared Personal Practice (.87); Supportive Conditions—Relationships (.82); Supportive Conditions—Structures (.88); and a one-factor solution (.97).

The latest analysis also provided an opportunity to review descriptive statistics for each item. Mean scores for the measure resulted in a high of 3.27 within the Collective Learning and Application dimension (i.e., *school staff is committed to programs that enhance learning*) to a low of 2.74 within the Shared Personal Practice dimension (i.e., *the staff provide feedback to peers related to instructional practices*). Subsequent studies have provided ongoing validation of this tool.[1]

The developers of the assessment determined that one important aspect of PLCs was missing from the original instrument—the collection, interpretation, and use of data in order to focus improvement efforts. The importance of this practice in learning communities is supported by Hord and Hirsh's (2008) assertion that "staff learning precedes student learning, and its focus derives from the study of both student and staff data that reveal specific needs. Thus, the staff engages in intentional and collegial learning aligned with needs and goals determined by data" (p. 29).

Specific items related to data are now integrated within each of the PLC dimensions. The *Professional Learning Community Assessment-Revised*

(PLCA-R) now serves as an even more powerful formal diagnostic tool for identifying school-level practices that support intentional professional learning.

The revised PLCA continues to provide perceptions of the staff relating to shared and supportive leadership, shared values and vision, collective learning and application, shared personal practice, and supportive conditions. The revised assessment also uses the same 4-point Likert scale ranging from 1 (Strongly Disagree) to 4 (Strongly Agree) as the original measure (see Table 4.1).

To verify the relevance of the seven new statements directly addressing a school's utilization of data, we solicited responses to an Expert Opinion Questionnaire from educators who had knowledge of the original PLCA measure or attributes of PLCs. The panel of experts consisted of school administrators and teachers, district and regional education supervisory personnel, university faculty and staff, educational consultants, and doctoral students studying PLCs. The PLCA revision process also sought feedback from several researchers and doctoral students who had utilized the measure.

The Expert Opinion Questionnaire had respondents rate proposed measure statements in terms of their *relevance* to data practices within a PLCA.

The 3-point rating scale included the following responses:

- H/(3) = high level of importance and relevance to PLCA instrument revision.
- M/(2) = medium level of importance and relevance to PLCA instrument revision.
- L/(1) = low level of importance and relevance to PLCA instrument revision.

Thus, the proposed items were assessed in terms of the importance and relevance to data use and the appropriate fit within the PLCA dimensions.

Findings from the Expert Opinion Questionnaire resulted in 51 usable surveys in which the seven items were rated, on the 3-point scale. Responses from experts were overwhelmingly positive and indicated the feasibility of utilizing the PLCA-R to assess data-related practices within the PLC dimensions.

Collectively, ratings ranged from a high of 2.94 (i.e., *staff collaboratively analyze evidence of student learning as critical data for improving teaching and learning*) to a low of 2.69 (i.e., *data are organized in a way to provide easy access to staff*). Overall, panel member ratings resulted in inclusion of all seven proposed items in the PLCA revision.

Table 4.1 Professional Learning Community Assessment-Revised (PLCA-R)

Directions:

This questionnaire assesses your perceptions about your principal, staff, and stakeholders based on the dimensions of a professional learning community (PLC) and related attributes. This questionnaire contains a number of statements about practices that occur in some schools. Read each statement and then use the scale to select the scale point that best reflects your personal degree of agreement with the statement. Shade the appropriate oval provided to the right of each statement. Be certain to select only one response for each statement. Comments after each dimension section are optional.

Key Terms:
- Principal: Principal, not associate or assistant principal
- Staff/Staff Members : All adult staff directly associated with curriculum, instruction, and assessment of students
- Stakeholders: Parents and community members

Scale: 1 = Strongly Disagree (SD)
           2 = Disagree (D)
           3 = Agree (A)
           4 = Strongly Agree (SA)

STATEMENTS		SCALE		
Shared and Supportive Leadership	SD	D	A	SA
1. Staff members are consistently involved in discussing and making decisions about most school issues.	0	0	0	0
2. The principal incorporates advice from staff members to make decisions.	0	0	0	0
3. Staff members have accessibility to key information.	0	0	0	0
4. The principal is proactive and addresses areas where support is needed.	0	0	0	0
5. Opportunities are provided for staff members to initiate change.	0	0	0	0
6. The principal shares responsibility and rewards for innovative actions.	0	0	0	0
7. The principal participates democratically with staff sharing power and authority.	0	0	0	0
8. Leadership is promoted and nurtured among staff members.	0	0	0	0
9. Decision making takes place through committees and communication across grade and subject areas.	0	0	0	0
10. Stakeholders assume shared responsibility and accountability for student learning without evidence of imposed power and authority.	0	0	0	0
11. Staff members use multiple sources of data to make decisions about teaching and learning.	0	0	0	0

COMMENTS:

Table 4.1 *(continued)*

STATEMENTS	SCALE			
Shared Values and Vision	SD	D	A	SA
12. A collaborative process exists for developing a shared sense of values among staff.	0	0	0	0
13. Shared values support norms of behavior that guide decisions about teaching and learning.	0	0	0	0
14. Staff members share visions for school improvement that have undeviating focus on student learning.	0	0	0	0
15. Decisions are made in alignment with the school's values and vision.	0	0	0	0
16. A collaborative process exists for developing a shared vision among staff.	0	0	0	0
17. School goals focus on student learning beyond test scores and grades.	0	0	0	0
18. Policies and programs are aligned to the school's vision.	0	0	0	0
19. Stakeholders are actively involved in creating high expectations that serve to increase student achievement.	0	0	0	0
20. Data are used to prioritize actions to reach a shared vision.	0	0	0	0

COMMENTS:

STATEMENTS	SCALE			
Collective Learning and Application	SD	D	A	SA
21. Staff members work together to seek knowledge, skills, and strategies and apply this new learning to their work.	0	0	0	0
22. Collegial relationships exist among staff members that reflect commitment to school improvement efforts.	0	0	0	0
23. Staff members plan and work together to search for solutions to address diverse student needs.	0	0	0	0
24. A variety of opportunities and structures exist for collective learning through open dialogue.	0	0	0	0
25. Staff members engage in dialogue that reflects a respect for diverse ideas that lead to continued inquiry.	0	0	0	0
26. Professional development focuses on teaching and learning.	0	0	0	0
27. School staff members and stakeholders learn together and apply new knowledge to solve problems.	0	0	0	0
28. School staff members are committed to programs that enhance learning.	0	0	0	0
29. Staff members collaboratively analyze multiple sources of data to assess the effectiveness of instructional practices.	0	0	0	0
30. Staff members collaboratively analyze student work to improve teaching and learning.	0	0	0	0

COMMENTS:

Table 4.1 *(continued)*

STATEMENTS	SCALE			
Shared Personal Practice	SD	D	A	SA
31. Opportunities exist for staff members to observe peers and offer encouragement.	0	0	0	0
32. Staff members provide feedback to peers related to instructional practices.	0	0	0	0
33. Staff members informally share ideas and suggestions for improving student learning.	0	0	0	0
34. Staff members collaboratively review student work to share and improve instructional practices.	0	0	0	0
35. Opportunities exist for coaching and mentoring.	0	0	0	0
36. Individuals and teams have the opportunity to apply learning and share the results of their practices.	0	0	0	0
37. Staff members regularly share student work to guide overall school improvement.	0	0	0	0

COMMENTS:

STATEMENTS	SCALE			
Supportive Conditions—Relationships	SD	D	A	SA
38. Caring relationships exist among staff and students that are built on trust and respect.	0	0	0	0
39. A culture of trust and respect exists for taking risks.	0	0	0	0
40. Outstanding achievement is recognized and celebrated regularly in our school.	0	0	0	0
41. School staff and stakeholders exhibit a sustained and unified effort to embed change into the culture of the school.	0	0	0	0
42. Relationships among staff members support honest and respectful examination of data to enhance teaching and learning.	0	0	0	0

COMMENTS:

STATEMENTS	SCALE			
Supportive Conditions—Structures	SD	D	A	SA
43. Time is provided to facilitate collaborative work.	0	0	0	0
44. The school schedule promotes collective learning and shared practice.	0	0	0	0
45. Fiscal resources are available for professional development.	0	0	0	0
46. Appropriate technology and instructional materials are available to staff.	0	0	0	0

COMMENTS:

Table 4.1 *(continued)*

STATEMENTS	SCALE			
	SD	D	A	SA
47. Resource people provide expertise and support for continuous learning.	0	0	0	0
48. The school facility is clean, attractive, and inviting.	0	0	0	0
49. The proximity of grade level and department personnel allows for ease in collaborating with colleagues.	0	0	0	0
50. Communication systems promote a flow of information among staff members.	0	0	0	0
51. Communication systems promote a flow of information across the entire school community including: central office personnel, parents, and community members.	0	0	0	0
52. Data are organized and made available to provide easy access to staff members.	0	0	0	0

COMMENTS:

Table 4.2 provides comments from researchers, doctoral students, and practitioners on the usability and feasibility of the PLCA measure to assess school practices relating to the dimensions and attributes of a PLC.

An additional enhancement to the PLCA-R format, made in response to user feedback, is a Comment section at the conclusion of each of the dimension sections. This revision provides a means for respondents to offer qualitative data within each dimension that can enrich understanding of quantitative data and guide future action.

When analyzing PLCA-R results, descriptive statistics are beneficial in determining the strength of the dimensions, as well as reviewing teacher responses for each individual item. Given that PLCA-R items illustrate actual school-level practices, analysis of the measure should incorporate a review of individual items to determine the strength and weaknesses of practices deemed essential within a PLC.

TEACHER EFFICACY BELIEFS SCALE-COLLECTIVE FORM

When analyzing the progress of schools along the PLC continuum, it is essential to determine the level of effectiveness of organizational aspects, including collective efficacy. Teachers in PLC schools have strong collective efficacy beliefs in their capacity to promote student academic success (Olivier, 2001). Furthermore, Hargreaves (1995) emphasizes that working together in a PLC serves as a way of building relationships and collective resolve and as a source of learning.

Table 4.2   Feedback on the Professional Learning Community Assessment

Role	Comment
High school principal	The measure served to provide "data that . . . is highly pertinent to the everyday lives of a building principal."
Principal	"I conducted the PLCA this past fall. . . . I am very excited to see that you are contemplating adding the data component to each of the strands of the PLCs."
Principal	"The PLCA supported the central intent of my study quite well because of its robust alignment with my conceptual framework on PLCs . . . [the measure] served as a user-friendly, yet rigorous quantitative component in a mixed-method case study . . . its language was also the language of the PLC literature, the language that emerged in focus groups with my participants; in relation to the structure of the measure—some teachers indicated that the four-point Likert, absent the often-seen neutral option, caused them to think extensively about their responses . . . and that after thinking deeply about an item, they were glad they were forced to commit to a positive or negative response"; "the PLCA gave me a clear, initial picture of the extent to which our organization shows characteristics and supportive conditions of a PLC . . . overall, the PLCA appeared to paint a profile of our school that was congruent with and confirmatory of the qualitative data I collected via focus group interviews, individual interviews, open-ended, anonymous questionnaire, and document analysis."
Researcher	Using the PLCA as checkpoints, the measure provided a sense of "the school's progress towards becoming a professional learning community. . . . I believe the findings represent an accurate measure of what is really going on there."
Regional educational staff member	"I really like the new items and think they are a good addition to the existing survey. The new items support what our office [regional education office] suggests about using data to inform instruction."
Teacher	The measure served to provide an analysis of specific aspects of interest within the school. . . . "The leadership questions helped me to analyze how and if teachers felt that they were empowered to not only work as a collaborative community, but also to make or even suggest changes in their teaching practices."
Teacher	Regarding the quality of the PLCA . . . "the instrument was the centerpiece to my research study . . . as it allowed me to draw some very interesting conclusions. I found that the measure . . . helped me to tease out the nuances of how teachers collaborated and if they felt empowered by the collaborative experience."

As our knowledge base about the development of PLCs increased, our research team began to explore related variables within the culture of schools operating in this way. We analyzed data from individual interviews, focus groups, and school and classroom observations as a way to deepen understanding of how schools progress from initiation to implementation to sustainability.

Specifically, we wanted to understand how school staffs come to assume collective responsibility for student learning. Initial investigations led us to examine the reciprocal relationships between collective efficacy and leadership capacity within a PLC in more detail (Olivier & Hipp, 2006).

Our mixed methodology study revealed significant positive correlations among subgroup scales measuring leadership capacity, collective efficacy, and PLC dimensions.

Based on these results, we offer a second organizational measure, the *Teacher Efficacy Beliefs Scale-Collective Form* (TEBS-C) as a tool for assessing teachers' perceptions about their collective efficacy to organize and carry out tasks within their school environment (see Table 4.3; Olivier, 2001).

This one-dimensional 10-item measure has been empirically validated and shown to be a reliable measure of the strength of teachers' collective efficacy beliefs ($r = .96$). The means for the scale ranged from a high on *maintaining a school environment in which students feel good about themselves* ($M = 3.38$; $SD = .615$) to a low on *providing input in making important school decisions* ($M = 2.84$; $SD = .667$).

The validation study provided support for the TEBS-C as a unique measure of teacher collective efficacy as an organizational-level construct (Olivier, 2001). The tool offers an opportunity to examine an additional data set for assessing PLC-related variables within the context of the teaching and learning environment.

Meeting the needs of all students and providing optimum learning opportunities for students and staff is the focus of PLCs. The incorporation of the TEBS-C into a comprehensive analysis of PLCs provides insight into perceptions among staff regarding their capabilities to positively impact student learning. Subsequent findings have reinforced the need to study collective efficacy and leadership capacity as organizational variables evident in PLCs (Weber & Hipp, 2008). Educational leaders are urged to recognize the importance of collective efficacy as a concept within schools reculturing as PLCs (Olivier & Hipp, 2006).

In addition to incorporating the results of the TEBS-C and the PLCA-R, our research indicates the importance of leadership capacity in improving outcomes for students.

Our ongoing inquiry identified the Leadership Capacity School Survey (LCSS) developed by Lambert (2003) as a third measure of conditions that exist in schools progressing as PLCs. Although the LCSS is not included in this book, we believe it is a valuable tool for assessing the existence of shared and supportive leadership in schools (Lambert, 2003).

Figure 4.3 Teacher Efficacy Belief Scale-Collective Form (TEBS-C)

Directions: This survey requests that you make judgments about the *collective strength of beliefs of faculty members at your school* in their capabilities to organize and successfully carry out work tasks. Assess the strengths of faculty beliefs, consider the faculty's collective abilities within the context of your *current* school. Consider job roles and responsibilities, available resources and support, current policies, help from colleagues, and so on. Considering the faculty in your school as a whole, for each item, use the scale provided. Shade the appropriate oval provided to the right of each statement that best reflects your view.

STRENGTH OF FACULTY COLLECTIVE BELIEFS SCALE:
  1 = *Weak Beliefs* in our capabilities (WB)
  2 = *Somewhat Strong Beliefs* in our capabilities (SSB)
  3 = *Strong Beliefs* in our capabilities (SB)
  4 = *Very Strong Beliefs* in our capabilities (VSB)

The strength of our faculty's *collective beliefs* in our capabilities to . . .	WB	SSB	SB	VSB
1. carry out decisions and plans designed for school-wide improvement.	0	0	0	0
2. produce high levels of learning with our students.	0	0	0	0
3. create ways to improve the school environment.	0	0	0	0
4. maintain effective communication with parents and the larger community.	0	0	0	0
5. support each other in addressing new policies, rules, and regulations.	0	0	0	0
6. maintain a school environment in which students feel good about themselves.	0	0	0	0
7. provide input in making important school decisions.	0	0	0	0
8. effectively communicate with the school administration.	0	0	0	0
9. work with disadvantaged and troublesome students.	0	0	0	0
10. manage student misbehavior.	0	0	0	0

Source: Olivier, D. F. (2001). *Teacher personal and school culture characteristics in effective schools: Toward a model of a professional learning community.* Unpublished doctoral dissertation, Louisiana State University.

For detailed information on development and validation of the referenced instruments, including reliability and validity analyses, refer to the respective sources cited for each measure.

In our experience, using multiple measures of such progress yielded new insights into staff perceptions of PLC school-level practices, as well as evidence of levels of collective efficacy and leadership capacity.

USING DIALOGUE IN EXAMINING OUR DATA

How, then, might schools use the tools described to create learning communities that enhance student learning? The answer lies not simply in the collection and sharing of perceptual data, but in opportunities for structured dialogue about the results. Insights emerge from such dialogue around individual viewpoints, experiences, and reasons for discrepancies across ratings. Numbers alone rarely tell the story, and rich dialogue within a culture built upon trust and shared responsibility can contribute significantly to the development of a PLC.

Chris Argyris (1990), a pioneer in the study of dialogue, recommends a balance of inquiry and advocacy. This requires inquiry into others' perceptions, as well as presenting one's own thinking. Ideally, what ensues is a genuine sense of curiosity, most evident through probing and questioning. Over time, participants are more likely to let go of some of their deepseated beliefs and assumptions, build trust, expand their ways of thinking based on the experience and views of others, and establish relationships that promote integrity of action. Clarity around conflicting views and implications for practice become evident.

Bohm (1996) proposes that breakdowns in effectiveness of team and organizational learning are fueled by differences that perpetuate rigid ways of thinking. This is often evident in the beliefs and assumptions educators bring to the table. Until staff members reveal their own thoughts and actively listen to one another to come to some common understanding, their *mental models* (i.e., maps of one's thinking based on experiences) restrict an openness to learn and consider varying viewpoints.

Margaret Arbuckle noted the impact that honest and forthright staff interactions have on school culture:

> As educators—designers for learning, we have come to understand that some school cultures stimulate and promote learning. Others stifle it. You can feel the difference as soon as you walk into a school. Culture is rooted deeply in people. It is embodied in their attitudes, values, and skills, which in turn stem from their personal backgrounds, from their life experiences, and from the communities they belong to. (Senge et al., 2000, p. 325)

In order to address areas of greatest need, as revealed through dialogue, staff need to listen to the voices and experiences of *all* staff as they develop priorities, design next steps, and engage in immediate action. Individuals are often surprised at the differences in their perceptions regarding what the data seem to be telling them.

Several options, including both quantitative and qualitative methods, can be used to analyze interacting variables including the PLCA-R, TEBS-C, PLCO, LCSS, on-site school and classroom observations, and structured dialogue experiences. The selection of one or more measures offers opportunities for an in-depth and comprehensive study of schools seeking deliberate and carefully constructed learning for adults in order to produce better results for students (Hord & Hirsh, 2008).

More recently, Wellman and Lipton (2004) contend, "At the most fundamental level, dialogue is a process of listening and speaking to understand each other's ideas, assumption, beliefs and values. To understand others does not imply agreement or disagreement with their viewpoints. Dialogue seeks and explores the layers of meaning within ideas" (p. 39).

Moreover, "Data-driven dialogue is a collective process designed to create shared understanding of issues and events using information from many different sources" (Wellman & Lipton, 2004, p. 41).

The various measures provide for multiple data collection methods to assess and analyze the progress of schools seeking to function as productive PLCs. With PLCs as a viable infrastructure for sustainable school improvement, these multiple measures and processes offer options for continual assessment and analysis. "The use of data can make an enormous difference in school reform efforts by helping schools see how to improve school processes and student learning" (Bernhardt, 2004, p. 3). Unless data are revealed and processed, ways of thinking will not change, common ground will not be established, and actions will be limited in their effectiveness or misguided altogether.

The following steps provide an example of a process designed to engage staff in dialogue about perceptual data and to make decisions about those data:

- Gather the staff in small, mixed groups across grade and subject areas.
- Distribute perception survey results (e.g., PLCA-R, TEBS-C).
- Initiate a structured dialogue, allowing every person in the group an opportunity to share the rationale behind their ratings, present related evidence, and be heard without interruption.
- Encourage discrepant views and invite questions for the purpose of clarity and insight through an open and focused dialogue.
- Establish a safety net. Urge suspending judgments of others' thoughts and ideas, help participants identify similarities and differences, and examine how their *lived* practices affect the school culture and student learning.
- Structure multiple opportunities for dialogue so conversations do not take place in a single event, but as an ongoing process, engaging staff in continuous conversations in a variety of situations and venues at the team, school, and district levels.
- Maintain and update plans for implementation and monitoring. This process improves communication, links understanding with imple-

mentation, and serves to solve problems that culminate in shared meaning and purposeful action.

Several sources provide direction for engaging others in dialogue to create and sustain PLCs (Patterson, Grenny, McMillan, & Switzler, 2002; Senge, Kleiner, Roberts, Ross, & Smith, 1994; Senge et al., 2000; Wheatley, 2002). These sources describe ways to explore individuals' thinking, as well as their assumptions based on personal experiences that ultimately affect organizational learning and growth.

Creating the supportive conditions for dialogue, whether in analyzing data or in other staff interactions, is a critical aspect of developing a truly collaborative culture. Such a culture fosters the capacity to build mature and sustainable learning communities.

Change that begins with oneself, and ideally results in organizational change, comes from acknowledging our own beliefs and assumptions and inviting others to challenge our thinking while we challenge theirs.

Guidance can be taken from Paulo Freire (1970) who wrote in his landmark book, *Pedagogy of the Oppressed*, "We cannot be truly human apart from communication . . . to impede communication is to reduce people to the status of things" (p. 123).

5

Diagnostic
and Planning Tools

Jane Bumpers Huffman and Kristine Kiefer Hipp

This chapter familiarizes readers with informal instruments that support the formal diagnostic tools presented in Chapter 4. These less formal tools assist faculty and school administrators in their efforts to dialogue about dimensions of a PLC existing in a school, to create plans for fostering an instructional culture, and to structure next steps in developing a PLC.

The tools include

- the PLCO.
- the Professional Learning Community-Innovation Configuration Map (PLC-ICM).
- the External Support Systems-Innovation Configuration Map (ESS-ICM).
- the Professional Learning Community Developmental Rubric (PL-CDR).
- an Initial Plan for Creating PLCs.

Table 5.1 illustrates the tools, preferred individual or group application, and the purposes that guide the use of each tool. The term *preferred* is intentional because the authors recommend the use of these tools in the order presented. However, each school is faced with its own unique needs; therefore, this order may change if necessary.

The PLCO, as included in Chapter 3 as a conceptual description of the phases of change in a PLC, serves as a framework for the PLCA-R in Chapter 4 and the tools included in this chapter. Moreover, the PLCA-R provided

Table 5.1   Informal Professional Learning Community Tools

Tools	Purposes
PLCO (Facilitator led)	Illustrates practices identified through research that promote school efforts under each of the five dimensions of a PLC and phases of change
PLC-ICM and ESS-ICM (individual or small group)	Actions are suggested in each phase of change for each PLC dimension and critical attribute
PLCDR (individual and small group dialogue)	Reflect on the school's culture to delineate the progression of specific school-level practices that reflect each dimension of a PLC through each level of change
Initial Plan for Creating PLCs (small group)	Define goals and consider the current phase of implementation of each PLC dimension and related factors; plan next steps, develop an implementation timeline, and identify persons responsible for achieving each step

ESS-ICM, External Support Systems-Innovation Configuration Map; PLC, professional learning community; PLCDR, Professional Learning Community Developmental Rubric; Professional Learning Community-Innovation Configuration Map, PLC-ICM; PLCO, Professional Learning Community Organizer

the background for the development of the PLCDR. This rubric determines the progression of specific school-level practices that reflect each dimension through the levels of change as discussed by Fullan (1985).

INNOVATION CONFIGURATION MAPS

As administrators and staff work to assess their progress related to incorporating the learning community concept within their school, we find it helpful to clarify what this intervention looks like in practice.

Hall and Hord (2006) explain the Innovation Configuration Map that describes both the expected ideas of the change as well as the variations of the change that are evident in classrooms. This visual takes the form of a chart or matrix with the variations identified for each of the components of the change or innovation. These distinguishing practices allow the administrators and staff to discover where their actions fall on this continuum.

As administrators and staff use the PLC-ICM, it will become clear what actions are needed to move to the next variation in the development of a learning community (see Table 5.2). Thus, progress related to each PLC dimension can be assessed and next steps identified to help sustain the innovation.

Although the PLC-ICM is generally used by staff to assess their collective relationship to the change, the tool can also be used by teachers for individual review to guide future practice. Teachers will find it helpful to

Table 5.2 Professional Learning Community-Innovation Configuration Map (PLC-ICM)

Dimensions	Not Initiating	Initiating	Implementing	Sustaining
Shared and Supportive Leadership				
Information sharing and decision making	Administrators hold information and make decisions in isolation.	Administrators determine what information to share and with whom; selected staff are involved in decision making.	Administrators share most information with all staff and many decisions include most of the staff.	Information is available to all staff; administrators consistently involve staff in broad-based decision making.
Authority and responsibility	Staff authority and responsibility are limited to daily issues of classroom teaching and learning.	Administrators offer increased authority and responsibility and nurture selected staff around teaching and learning issues at classroom and school levels.	Administrators involve and nurture all staff around teaching and learning issues at classroom and school levels.	Administrators and staff share authority and responsibility around issues of teaching and learning at all levels.
Commitment and accountability	Staff do not hold themselves accountable for student learning.	Staff perceive themselves as accountable for student learning.	Staff hold themselves accountable for student learning.	Staff are committed to and accountable for student learning.
Shared Values and Vision				
Values	Administrators and individual staff members hold personal values about teaching and learning, but do not voice these to others.	Administrators and individual staff members hold personal values about teaching and learning, and voice these to a few selected colleagues.	Administrators and individual staff members hold personal values about teaching and learning and share these with all colleagues in open discussion.	Administrators and staff members use their personal values about teaching and learning as the foundation for developing shared values to guide school decisions.

Table 5.2 *(continued)*

Dimensions	Not Initiating	Initiating	Implementing	Sustaining
Focus	Administrators and staff address multiple areas of teaching and learning; some, but not all, areas focus on student learning; state and federal mandated assessments are not utilized.	Small groups of staff work together to address one or more areas of teaching and learning; most areas focus on student learning; student learning measures are not aligned to state and federal mandated assessments.	Staff agree on priority areas for teaching and learning; all priorities focus on high expectations for student learning; student learning measures are limited to state and federal mandated assessments.	Staff agree on priority areas for teaching and learning; all priorities focus on high expectations for student learning; student learning measures include, but are not limited to, state and federal mandated assessments.
Vision	The school district has a vision or mission statement, but no vision or mission statement exists for the school.	Staff are involved in a process to define the vision for the school; the vision is not used as a basis for decision making.	Staff are involved in a process to define the vision for the school; it is used as a basis for decision making.	Staff are involved in a process to define a shared vision; it is routinely used as a decision-making template for aligning policies, programs, and norms of behavior.

Collective Learning and Application

Collaboration	Staff seldom engage in discussions that focus on student data.	Staff engage in discussions that begin to address data related to student needs; continuous inquiry is inconsistently related to identified student needs.	Staff begin to engage in data-driven dialogue and share diverse ideas that lead to continuous inquiry related to identified student needs.	Staff engage in purposeful dialogue, share diverse ideas, engage in continuous inquiry, and provide solutions to identified student needs.

Table 5.2 *(continued)*

Dimensions	Not Initiating	Initiating	Implementing	Sustaining
Planning and problem solving	Staff work in isolation to plan and solve problems related to student and adult learning.	Staff work individually and with selected peers to plan and solve problems related to student and adult learning.	Staff work in purposeful learning teams to plan and solve problems related to student and adult learning.	Staff work across the school community to plan and solve problems related to student and adult learning.
Knowledge, skills, and strategies	Staff rarely work together to seek knowledge, skills, or strategies to improve practice.	Staff work together to seek knowledge, skills, and strategies to improve practice.	Staff work together in multiple ways (teams, departments, committees, etc.) to seek knowledge, skills, and strategies to improve practice.	Staff consistently work together and involve the school community in purposeful action aligned with shared knowledge, skills, and strategies to improve practice.

Shared Personal Practice

Observation	Staff do not observe one another teaching.	Some staff informally observe others teaching at arranged times during the school day.	Most staff regularly observe each other, formally and informally, at arranged times during the school day.	Staff observe each other, formally and informally, embedded throughout the school day.
Review and feedback	Staff do not review each other's work or offer feedback related to teaching.	Some staff review work and offer informal feedback and encouragement.	Most staff regularly review work and offer formal and informal feedback that encourages change of practice.	Staff regularly review student work and offer substantive feedback that changes attitudes and practice.

Table 5.2   *(continued)*

Dimensions	Not Initiating	Initiating	Implementing	Sustaining
Sharing outcomes of practice	Staff do not share knowledge and personal practice.	Some staff work collaboratively to share knowledge and practice.	Most staff collaborate to share knowledge and outcomes of practice to improve student learning.	A collaborative culture exists that supports staff in sharing knowledge and outcomes of practice to improve student learning.
Mentoring and coaching	Formal and informal mentoring and coaching systems do not exist.	Some staff are involved in informal mentoring and coaching.	Most staff use both formal and informal systems of assistance including mentoring and coaching.	Mentoring and coaching systems are in place to support teacher practice related to improving student learning.

Supportive Conditions—Structures

Dimensions	Not Initiating	Initiating	Implementing	Sustaining
Communication systems	Accurate and meaningful communication is not regularly shared with staff.	Accurate and meaningful communication is often shared with staff.	Accurate and meaningful two-way communication flows between administration and staff.	Communication systems promote a flow of information across the entire school community.
Technology systems	Appropriate technology and instructional materials seldom meet the needs of staff to enhance student learning.	Appropriate technology and instructional materials usually meet the needs of staff to enhance student learning.	Staff are involved in the selection of appropriate technology and instructional materials that meet the needs of staff to enhance student learning.	Staff and administrators use data to determine appropriate technology and instructional materials that meet the needs of staff to enhance student learning.
Resources (personnel, facilities, time, and money)	Resources are not sufficient to promote staff and student learning.	The need for adequate resources is considered to promote staff and student learning.	Resources are appropriate, in most cases, to increase staff and student learning.	Innovative efforts across the school community result in garnering resources that impact continual staff and student learning.

Table 5.2 *(continued)*

Dimensions	Not Initiating	Initiating	Implementing	Sustaining
Supportive Conditions—Relationships				
Trust and respect	Efforts do not exist that promote change in the culture of the school; staff work in isolated units with limited personal interactions.	Some efforts exist that promote change in the culture of the school; staff engage in limited interactions and seldom take risks.	Staff and students are committed to promote change in the culture of the school; interactions reveal substantive sharing and risk-taking.	Interactions across the entire school community promote sustained and unified efforts through risk-taking to embed change in the culture of the school.
Recognition and celebration	Achievement is rarely recognized or celebrated; a sense of caring is seldom apparent in the school.	Some efforts exist to recognize and celebrate achievement; caring relationships are apparent.	Achievement is regularly recognized and celebrated. A caring culture exists.	The entire school community promotes a caring culture that recognizes and celebrates achievements.

use the map for self-reflection, as well as for peer observations within classrooms.

The concept of a PLC in this volume involves the *professional* staff in the school, which generally includes administrators, teachers, reading specialists, literacy coaches, school counselors, social workers, and other specialists. However, professionals can be even more successful working to increase student learning by attaining relevant resources external from the school, such as central office personnel, parents and families, and community members that comprise the entire school system. Therefore, we add these external support systems in Table 5.3 for staff to use to extend their reach in obtaining critical resources for the teaching and learning process.

Table 5.3   External Support Systems—Innovation Configuration Map (ESS-ICM)

External Support Systems	Not initiating	Initiating	Implementing	Sustaining
Central office	Central office personnel provide minimal direction, resources, and support for school improvement efforts.	Central office personnel provide adequate direction, resources, and support for school improvement efforts.	Central office personnel participate consistently in providing direction, resources, and support for school improvement efforts.	Central office personnel play an integral role in building capacity within and across schools related to direction, resources, and support for school improvement efforts.
Parents and families	Parents and families minimally participate in decision making and issues related to student learning, school improvement, and extra-curricular activities.	Some parents and families participate in decision making and issues related to student learning, school improvement, and extra-curricular activities.	Many parents and families participate in decision making and issues related to student learning, school improvement, and extra-curricular activities.	Parents and families are regularly involved in decision making and participate meaningfully around issues related to student learning, school improvement, and extra-curricular activities.
Community members	Community members play a limited role in supporting student learning, school improvement, and extra-curricular activities.	Some community members play a role in supporting student learning, school improvement, and extra-curricular activities.	Many community members play a role in supporting student learning, school improvement, and extra-curricular activities.	Community members play a significant role in supporting student learning, school improvement, and extra-curricular activities.

PROFESSIONAL LEARNING
COMMUNITY DEVELOPMENT RUBRIC

The PLCDR enables school and district staff to identify and delineate practices that build on the more formal diagnostic purposes of the PLCA-R (see Table 4.1).

When using the PLCDR in schools and districts, staff indicate how the school currently operates along a continuum related to the most appropriate phase of change (Hipp & Huffman, 2007). Ideally, staff members meet at a whole school level to complete the instrument and then share their individual ratings in small groups by providing specific evidence of the practices in their school. Dialogue that follows generally allows for the expression of alternative, even opposing viewpoints.

In effective dialogue, difficult issues surface, and are identified, and solutions drive next steps related to school or district goals. Ongoing conversations occur frequently and in numerous venues, such as in teams and at the department, school, and district levels. See the PLCDR in Table 5.4.

Fullan's (1985) Phases of Change model including initiating-implementing-institutionalizing was also utilized and a fourth phase, *not initiating*, was added as many schools begin their change efforts at this level. Using parallel terms, we also note that Stoll, McMahon, and Thomas (2006) added *stifled* to reflect this phase to their descriptive conceptions of *starting*, *doing*, and *embedding* to further describe Fullan's phases. Finally, we have replaced Fullan's *institutionalizing* phase with *sustaining* to more accurately reflect the current literature on the change process and PLCs.

INITIAL PLAN FOR CREATING
A PROFESSIONAL LEARNING COMMUNITY

Another tool we use in our work with schools and other audiences is the Initial Plan for Creating a PLC. We find that unless the dialogue that begins after completing any of the formal or informal instruments leads to action, efforts are for naught. Insightful discussions often end with a flurry of undocumented and unorganized thoughts that never materialize.

Table 5.5 provides the template for future planning and an example of how to approach first steps.

To use this plan, staff members first assess formally or informally their school's specific phase of change related to the development of each dimension in the PLC structure. Then staff members identify the first steps including what to keep, what to stop, and what to start; the timeline; and the person(s) responsible. In the initial plan in Figure 5.2, the example for shared and supportive leadership is offered for guidance.

Because we suggest that each of the PLC dimensions and related factors be considered, addressing all areas at one time can be overwhelming. To better ensure your success in this process, consider limiting your focus to two or three primary areas. Consensus can be sought as to which areas, if addressed, will yield the highest leverage and success for students.

Table 5-4 Professional Learning Community Development Rubric (PLCDR)

Professional educators working collectively and purposefully to create and sustain a culture of learning for all students and adults.
The following dimensions are characteristics of academically successful professional learning communities.

Dimensions	Not Initiated	Initiation (starting)	Implementation (doing)	Institutionalization (embedding)
Shared and Supportive Leadership Administrators share power, authority, and decision making, while promoting and nurturing leadership. ☐	Leadership is held by school administrators; staff are not empowered around issues of teaching and learning. ☐	Pockets of leadership exist beyond school administrators; staff are nurtured and encouraged to take leadership roles. ☐	Leadership is prevalent across the school; staff share power, authority, and responsibility around issues of teaching and learning. ☐	Leadership and decision making are broad-based; empowerment exists around issues of teaching and learning; staff are committed and accountable. ☐
Shared Values and Vision The staff share visions that have an undeviating focus on student learning and support norms of behavior that guide decisions about teaching and learning. ☐	A school vision, values, and plan do not exist, or do not involve stakeholders; there is a lack of focus on student learning. ☐	Values and norms are espoused; a collaborative process exists for developing shared values and vision; some focus exists on student learning, but efforts are not aligned. ☐	Shared vision and a set of values exist that reflect high expectations for student learning; efforts are aligned. ☐	A shared vision and set of values is "lived" across the entire school community, and guide decisions, policies, and programs related to teaching and learning. ☐
Collective Learning and Application The staff share information and work collaboratively to plan, solve problems, and improve learning opportunities. ☐	Collective learning does not exist; staff does not show evidence of learning from one another to meet diverse student needs. ☐	Staff meet to share information and discuss issues of teaching and learning; staff begin to dialogue and act on their learning to meet diverse student needs. ☐	Staff meet regularly to collaborate and problem solve around teaching and learning; staff show evidence of learning from one another to meet diverse student needs. ☐	Staff share information and work together to seek new knowledge, skills, and strategies; staff apply new learning to their work, and search for solutions to address diverse student needs. ☐

Dimension				
Shared Personal Practice Peers meet and observe one another to provide feedback on instructional practices, to assist in student learning, and to increase human capacity. ☐	Staff work in isolation, do not observe one another, offer feedback, or share practices with one another. ☐	Some staff work collaboratively to observe and encourage one another, offer feedback, or share practices with one another. ☐	Staff work collaboratively, observe one another, offer feedback, and formally and informally share outcomes of new practices to improve student learning. ☐	Formal and informal mentoring and coaching programs exist; staff observe one another and provide feedback, staff regularly review student work together and share instructional practices. ☐
Supportive Conditions (Structures) include systems (communication and technology) resources (personnel, facilities, time, fiscal, and materials) to enable staff to meet and examine practices and student outcomes. ☐	Systems and resources are not sufficient to promote staff and student learning. ☐	The need for adequate systems and resources is considered to address staff and student learning. ☐	Systems and resources are appropriate, in most cases, to increase staff and student learning. ☐	Innovative efforts result in systems and resources that impact continual staff and student learning. ☐
Supportive Conditions (Relationships) include respect, trust, norms of critical inquiry and improvement, and positive, caring relationships among the entire school community. ☐	Efforts do not exist that promote change in the culture of the school, such as: caring, trust, respect, a sense of safety, and recognition and celebration of efforts and achievement. ☐	Some efforts exist that promote change in the culture of the school, such as: caring, trust, respect, a sense of safety, and recognition and celebration of efforts and achievement. ☐	Staff and students are committed to promote change in the culture of the school, such as: caring, trust, respect, a sense of safety, and recognition and celebration of efforts and achievement. ☐	The entire school community promotes sustained and unified efforts to take risks to embed change in the culture of the school, such as: caring, trust, respect, a sense of safety, and recognition and celebration of efforts and achievement. ☐

Table 5.5 Initial Plan for Creating a Professional Learning Community: Professional Learning Community Dimensions and Related Factors

Goal(s):

PLC Dimensions	Phase of Change Initiating, Implementing Sustaining	First Steps Keep/Stop/Start	Timeline	Person(s) Responsible
Shared and Supportive Leadership Administrators share power, authority, and decision making, while promoting and nurturing leadership.	Initiating	KEEP -School committees with co-chairs -Leadership Team	August August	-Principal -Committee Co-Chairs -Principal and Leadership Team
		-Leadership structure with department chairs	August	-Principal -Department Chairs
		STOP -Keeping people out of the loop	Sept	-School as a whole
		-Announcing decisions and holding people accountable without input	Sept/Oct	-Principal and Leadership Team
		START -Examine the role of the Leadership Team and how they can function to improve communication, elicit input, and share in decisions	Sept/Oct	-Principal and staff members
		-Redesign structures and increase opportunities for leadership	October	-Principal and staff members
Shared Values and Vision The staff share visions that have an undeviating focus on student learning, and support norms of behavior that guide decisions about teaching and learning.				

Table 5.5 *(continued)*

Goal(s):

PLC Dimensions	Phase of Change Initiating, Implementing Sustaining	First Steps Keep/Stop/Start	Timeline	Person(s) Responsible
Collective Learning and Application The staff share information and work collaboratively to plan, solve problems, and improve learning opportunities.				
Shared Personal Practice Peers meet and observe one another to provide feedback on instructional practices, to assist in student learning, and to increase human capacity.				
Supportive Conditions (Structures) include systems (communication and technology) resources (personnel, facilities, time, fiscal, and materials) to enable staff to meet and examine practices and student outcomes.				
Supportive Conditions (Relationships) include respect, trust, norms of critical inquiry and improvement, and positive, caring relationships among the entire school community.				
Collective Efficacy is the group members' perceptions of their collective ability to successfully complete a task.				

Table 5.5   *(continued)*

Goal(s):

PLC Dimensions	Phase of Change Initiating, Implementing Sustaining	First Steps Keep/Stop/Start	Timeline	Person(s) Responsible
Leadership Capacity is broad-based, skilled participation in the work of leadership regardless of role or position (Lambert, 2003).				
External Factors include parents, community, and central office personnel.				

Staff members begin to reflect on what to keep, that is, what is working. Next, they grapple with what they need to stop doing because currently there are either no benefits, or practices are actually interfering with the PLC the school is trying to create. Finally, they consider what actions to start even if they seem small. This begins the process of shared responsibility and accountability within established time parameters and specified assignments.

The number of dimensions and related factors addressed at one time is not the issue. It is most important to embed the *Initial Plan for Creating a PLC* into the school's improvement plan and determine what is realistically possible in the short term. If school staff choose to address all dimensions and related factors, they may be integrated over time into the school's long-range plan.

SUMMARY

In working with various audiences at all levels, we have found that these *five* informal tools (i.e., PLCO, PLC-ICM, ESS-ICM, PLCDR, and PLC-Initial Plan) offer flexibility as to the needs of staff and students. They provide structures for conversations that can be initiated and continued in many venues and provide insights representing the thinking of all staff members, thus giving voice to all and building ownership for establishing and sustaining PLCs.

Using the formal tools presented in Chapter 4 and the informal tools presented in this chapter results in a rich pool of information to generate deep conversation regarding PLCs. To move these data-driven conversations to the next step, Chapter 6 provides a structured process, which suggests purposeful teacher and administrator actions that guide teaching and learning.

6

+

The Professional
Teaching and Learning Cycle

A Strategy for Creating
Professional Learning Communities

D'Ette Fly Cowan

It comes as no accident that the word *learning* is positioned at the center of the term *professional learning community*, for a focus on learning lies at the core of schools that operate in this way. In such places, learning is a firmly entrenched expectation not only for students, but also for the adults responsible for student learning. In fact, learning on the part of the adults is considered a necessary precursor to learning on the part of students (Cowan, 2003).

The two words on either side of the word *learning* provide clarity about what the learning is focused on, as well as the context in which the learning occurs.

Professional indicates that the learning of adults draws on subject matter from well-regarded sources to make them more effective in their work. This term also suggests an expectation for high standards and continuous learning that promote public respect and confidence by constantly honing existing knowledge and skills and staying abreast of emerging promising practices.

The word *community* specifies the environment that supports the professional learning—one that nurtures trust, respect, and open dialogue about a shared vision and a strong, common commitment to student learning.

These three words, when considered separately, help us to recognize that a PLC is more than a popular three-word catchphrase for describing schools. Each word becomes an important aspect of the total phrase. When considered together, the words describe an *infrastructure* that supports and nurtures continuous learning and improvement on the part of adults to achieve increased student learning.

Previous chapters have described the five dimensions of a PLC, as well as formal and informal assessments of a school staff's current status in relation to each.

This chapter provides a process for creating (or strengthening) a community of professional learners among the instructional staff by focusing on a critical aspect of improving student outcomes: the alignment of curriculum, instruction, and assessment to state standards (Airasian, 2004; Cawelti, 2004; Kannapel & Clements, 2005; Marzano, 2003). It offers a structure for collaboration about teaching and learning and promotes continuous job-embedded professional development (Cowan, 2006; Hord & Sommers, 2008; Pankake & Moller, 2003). High levels of student learning become the ultimate shared goal, and strong professional relationships support continuous inquiry about existing and new instructional practices. It is a particularly powerful strategy for promoting two PLC dimensions described in previous chapters: collective learning and shared personal practice.

THE PROFESSIONAL TEACHING AND LEARNING CYCLE

The literature is rife with descriptions and characteristics of PLCs, but it does not provide much direction on how to create and sustain them. The Professional Teaching and Learning Cycle (PTLC), originally developed as a process for aligning curriculum, instruction, and assessment to state standards in a joint effort by the Charles A. Dana Center at the University of Texas at Austin and the SEDL (2005),[1] consists of six steps: (a) study, (b) select, (c) plan, (d) implement, (e) analyze, and (f) adjust (see Figure 6.1).

Following is a brief description of the purpose and processes within each step, as well as a brief vignette to give the reader an idea of how the PTLC might be implemented.

Step 1: Study

In this step, teachers work in grade-level, vertical, or departmental teams to examine and discuss student achievement data and learning expectations in selected state standards. Often the selection of standards for study is predicated by high or low student performance on annual or periodic standards-based assessments. The purpose of this collaboration is to develop a common understanding of

- the concepts and skills students need to know and have to meet the expectations in the standards.
- how the standards in a grade or course are assessed on state and local tests.

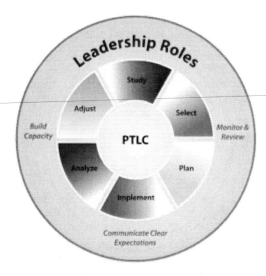

Figure 6.1.

- how the standards fit within a scope and sequence of the district curriculum (Cowan, Joyner, & Beckwith, 2008, p. 178).

Examining standards and objectives on which students perform at a high level helps identify strengths in the curriculum, instructional resources, and strategies. Similarly, examining standards and objectives on which students perform at a low level helps identify possible weaknesses in the curriculum, instructional resources, and strategies. Often these processes require paying close attention to the wording used in the standards and student learning expectations to determine critical concepts to be learned and skills to be mastered. Focusing attention on these concepts and skills helps build a shared understanding of how standards are connected across grade levels and subject areas.

Step 1 (Study) in Action   Principal Tate at Cimarron Middle School has organized a campus leadership team charged with primary responsibility for school improvement. The campus leadership team is composed of teacher representatives from each of the four core areas (i.e., math, reading/language arts, science, and social studies), as well as from fine arts, physical education, special education, and the Bilingual/English as a Second Language program. A district-level math coach and a district-level literacy coach who have curricular and instructional responsibilities complete the team.

The team meets on a regular basis each month to monitor implementation of the campus improvement plan and to deliberate on significant issues that emerge. The improvement plan supports the overall district plan and also addresses specific campus needs. In recent years, the team's shared norms have helped it come together by offering a range of perspectives on key improvement initiatives and by prioritizing school needs.

Now, at the beginning of the school year, the team examines the previous year's state test data and notes that student math performance is beginning to plateau. Team members come to realize that the school's current achievement level in math will not meet the state target at the end of the current year when performance standards increase. The team identifies the level of proficiency it wants students to attain on the next state assessment. Principal Tate is somewhat surprised, and gratified, to see that teachers' expectations in math achievement for the next school year exceed the minimum state level standards for math performance.

Later that week, Principal Tate and the math and literacy coaches meet with all the math teachers during their common planning period to discuss trends and patterns in math data over the past three years. The team identifies specific standards and objectives on which student performance has shown little or no improvement over that time period. The teachers agree that their instructional strategies need to be discussed, but not all of them are willing to make major changes in their classroom practices.

After collaborating with one another, the coaches develop a plan for helping the math teachers dig more deeply into the state standards to identify the concepts and skills required for student proficiency in specific objectives.

First, they have the teachers identify major concepts and prerequisite knowledge central to the objectives. This exercise helps them note key vocabulary terms embedded within the objectives, as well as specific instructional strategies that would best fit the vocabulary terms under consideration. The coaches then have the teachers identify skills students must develop to master the objectives.

After comparing the concepts and skills in specific standards and objectives at the grade levels below and after the grade they teach, the math teachers become more aware of how concepts and skills are progressively and intentionally built from grade to grade. From this discussion, the math coach describes how she can provide professional development in research-based strategies for teaching those skills.

Finally, the math coach directs teachers' attention to specific items on the state assessment on which the objectives are tested. The coach emphasizes the prerequisite and problem-solving skills required of students in order to demonstrate proficiency on the objectives.

Step 2: Select

In this step, teams investigate research-based strategies and needed resources to promote student mastery of the targeted standard(s). Teachers collaborate to

- identify effective research-based strategies and appropriate resources that will be used to support student learning of selected state standards.
- agree on assessment techniques that will be used to provide evidence of student learning (Cowan et al., 2008, p. 179).

This step requires teachers to determine whether strategies they have used in the past are supported in research and challenges them to adopt new and more effective strategies. As trust develops within teams, the teachers become more open to trying new strategies and reporting the outcomes to their colleagues.

Step 2 (Select) in Action   Following the meeting with the math teachers, Principal Tate asks the literacy and math coaches to confer to develop a plan for professional development that builds math teachers' capacity to provide effective instructional strategies on identified standards and learning objectives. The previous meeting with the teachers has provided valuable information about specific areas in which math teachers need a common understanding about what the standards and objectives require of students. The coaches are also becoming increasingly aware of teachers' pedagogical needs and how they can help increase teachers' instructional effectiveness in these areas.

The coaches examine the district's benchmark assessments to see how students are tested on the objectives throughout the school year. They discover a major discrepancy between the demands of the state assessment and how students are tested quarterly on local benchmarks. They set a date to discuss this inconsistency with the district's curriculum specialist in order to make needed changes on the local benchmark assessment. The math coach speculates that additional work will need to be done with math teachers to examine how students are tested on weekly or unit tests.

The literacy coach focuses on strategies for teaching key vocabulary terms identified previously by math teachers and makes special note of how (or whether) these terms have been introduced in the district's scope and sequence. She identifies three research-based strategies for teaching key terminology and helping students write cogent explanations for their problem solutions—a proficiency required on the state assessment.

Step 3: Plan

Teachers then collaborate to formally plan a lesson that incorporates selected research-based instructional strategies. They also agree on the type
of student work they will collect and share with one another as evidence
of student learning, as well as the criteria for measuring proficiency. In
collaboration, teachers

- develop a common formal plan outlining the lesson objectives (relevant to the standards), the materials to be used, the procedures, the
  time frame for the lesson, and the activities in which students will be
  engaged.
- decide what evidence of student learning will be collected during the
  implementation (Cowan et al., 2008, p. 179).

Planning the lesson collaboratively is a critical feature of the PTLC.
Through this process, teachers use their collective knowledge and experience to design a lesson that everyone understands and feels comfortable
teaching, to formulate one or more measures of proficiency, and to identify common student work to collect across classrooms as evidence of
learning.

Step 3 (Plan) in Action   The math teachers at each grade level then meet
to develop a common lesson that they agree to teach within a specified
period of time. They decide to use one of the new vocabulary strategies
they learned from the literacy coach.

Teachers first identify the major objectives of the lesson that are critical
to student proficiency in the standard and write these down. They also
decide on the assessment strategy they will use to determine the effectiveness of the lesson and formulate a simple rubric for judging student proficiency on key aspects of the assignment. They discuss the student work
they will bring back to the group once everyone has taught the lesson.

Because the concept they are teaching will require 4 days of instruction, the
teachers expand the agreed-on lesson to this longer time frame and decide on
two informal assessments and one formal assessment as evidence of lesson
effectiveness to bring back to the group for close examination.

Step 4: Implement

Teachers then teach the planned lesson, make note of successes and challenges, and collect evidence of student work. They

- deliver the lesson as planned within the specified time period.

- record results, especially noting where students struggled or where instruction did not achieve expected outcomes.
- collect the agreed-on evidence of student learning to take back to the collaborative planning team (Cowan et al., 2008, p. 179).

This step places the teacher in the role of an action researcher who collects data that reveal successes and challenges in the lesson. This process encourages active reflection to promote ongoing self-assessment and internal dialogue about the lesson as it was planned and presented.

Step 4 (Implement) in Action   Using the series of lesson plans developed together, the math teachers return to their classrooms and teach the lessons. During the lesson they note specific areas their students find particularly challenging or easy and record them. These notes will be useful when student work is examined in Step 5. The teachers use collaboratively developed informal and formal assessments and collect student work from these assessments.

Step 5: Analyze

In this step, teachers meet to examine the student work collected to serve as evidence of student understanding of the standards. Teachers work together to

- revisit and familiarize themselves with the targeted standards before analyzing student work.
- analyze a sampling of student work for evidence of student learning.
- discuss whether students have met the expectations outlined in the standards and make inferences about the strengths, weaknesses, and implications of instruction.
- identify what students know and what skills or knowledge needs to be strengthened in future lessons (Cowan et al., 2008, pp. 179–180).

The most important aspect of this step is the dialogue that occurs about lesson effectiveness as reflected in the student work. Whether conducted through formal or informal processes, the focus of examination is not on teacher evaluation, but rather on lesson effectiveness.

Step 5 (Analyze) in Action   At the specified time, the math teachers come back together to examine samples of student work. The math and literacy coaches also attend this meeting, primarily to lead the discussion and ask probing questions as teachers are learning the process. The literacy coach listens for indicators that teachers have provided a sound foundation on essential vocabulary for the lesson. The math coach is interested in hearing teacher perspectives about how the student work enhances development of critical math concepts and reflects effective pedagogy.

Although coaches are prepared to lead the discussion in the initial meetings, they realize that their presence at every meeting in the future will not be so essential as teachers become more adept in the process of analyzing student work.

The coaches have the math teachers shield the student's name from view on his or her work—by simply folding back the top of the paper. This helps prevent preconceived notions about individual student competency based on past achievement or other factors from creeping into the assessment of the work.

The math teachers next combine the student work from all the math teachers into one stack of papers. The coaches have the teachers review the objectives of the lesson as specified in Step 3. They also refer to the rubric they developed to ensure that indicators of proficiency are still appropriate.

The teachers review each piece of student work together and place it into one of three stacks: (a) those who excelled in meeting all the learning objectives; (b) those who are proficient in most of the learning objectives; and (c) those who are clearly off the mark in meeting the learning objectives. The coaches help prevent the conversation from drifting toward factors other than the work that is before the teachers.

Then, looking at each stack, the teachers identify the overall characteristics that are reflected in each of the three stacks and what elements of the commonly planned lesson might have influenced the student learning results. Teachers may want to speculate about anything that occurred in their classroom during the lesson that might have influenced results.

The teachers also examine each stack for any trends or patterns in strengths and errors and discuss what it would take to move student work in that stack to the next level. Although the focus of the conversation is on lesson effectiveness, the teachers realize they can use information in these stacks to group students for enrichment or additional instruction.

Step 6: Adjust

In this step, teachers reflect on the implications arising from the analysis of student work. They discuss alternative instructional strategies or modifications to the original strategy that may better promote student learning. In collaboration, teachers

- reflect on their common or disparate teaching experiences.
- consider and identify alternative instructional strategies for future instruction.
- refine and improve the lesson.
- determine when the instructional modifications will take place, what can be built into subsequent lessons, and what needs an additional targeted lesson (Cowan et al., 2008, p. 180).

Instruction is constantly evolving in this step as teachers design the most effective lessons possible. Follow-up instruction also becomes very strategic in nature as decisions are made about which students need additional instruction and how this instruction should be provided.

Step 6 (Adjust) in Action   The math and literacy coaches next guide the conversation toward possible changes that could be made in the lesson to increase its effectiveness. They also help the teachers see where small groups of students might be formed for immediate instruction on critical aspects of the learning objectives that were missed. In addition, they help the teachers plan how to integrate the missed objectives into future lessons. These measures increase the efficiency of the instructional program by targeting specific learning needs of students and reducing the number of students who need additional instruction. Throughout this process, the coaches communicate with Principal Tate and make recommendations for ways to continue to support teacher effectiveness.

The PTLC provides an ongoing, job-embedded strategy for increasing the alignment of instruction and assessment to state standards and local curriculum. It also provides a strategy for promoting a community of professional learners by fostering effective collaboration that promotes collective learning and shared personal practice. Furthermore, this process offers a means to focus professional development to provide continual support and assistance in building teachers' content and pedagogical knowledge and skills.

LEADERSHIP ROLES TO SUPPORT IMPLEMENTATION OF THE PROFESSIONAL TEACHING AND LEARNING CYCLE

Although the PTLC relates to the PLC dimensions of collective learning and application and shared personal practice, with a primary focus on classroom practice, responsibility for effective teaching is not limited to the classroom level. The PTLC requires ongoing collegial interactions and leadership support from district staff, principals, instructional coaches, and content specialists, particularly as teachers are learning to engage in this strategy.

Three essential leadership responsibilities are described next (Cowan et al., 2008).

Communicating Clear Expectations

Leaders communicate their own commitment to the implementation of the PTLC in what they say and do. Through words and actions, they communicate expectations that all staff will participate in the PTLC process and use it as a strategy to provide effective learning opportunities for students and build healthy professional relationships with their colleagues.

Building Capacity

In implementing the PTLC, leaders become more aware of staff members who need support and offer that support on a timely basis. They provide resources, such as time for collaboration, and support from instructional coaches and content specialists as needed. They become active in selection and participation in professional development to increase teacher capacity to deliver effective instruction and assess student progress appropriately.

Monitoring and Reviewing

Leaders consistently monitor the effectiveness of collaboration occurring within teams and intervene when needed by asking reflective questions, providing needed resources, and maintaining the focus on instructional improvement. They frequently and regularly monitor classroom instruction to determine whether research-based strategies are being used and their effect on student engagement.

BENEFITS OF THE PROFESSIONAL TEACHING AND LEARNING CYCLE

As a process for promoting the development of a PLC through alignment of the written, taught, and tested curriculum, the PTLC represents a practical and viable strategy for collaboration on teaching and learning, job-embedded professional development that impacts classroom practice, and leadership for the improvement of teaching and learning (Huie, Buttram, Deviney, Murphy, & Ramos, 2004). Explanations of each of these important strategies follow.

Collaboration on Teaching and Learning

Through collaboration on teaching and learning, the PTLC helps tear down territorial walls that prevent teachers from admitting their challenges and using their colleagues' expertise. Such collaboration fosters a clear sense of shared purpose and helps define roles and responsibilities. Teachers share and solve problems more readily and thereby become more certain and transparent about their practice. Interactions of this nature strengthen instructional program coherence, leading to increased student success.

Although structures for collaboration (e.g., grade-level and departmental groups) alone are not sufficient, they are very helpful in providing conditions under which authentic dialogue about teaching and learning can be realized. Even more important are norms of collaboration and collegiality that have a powerful effect on the quality and depth of such interactions (Tschannen-Moran, 2004).

As teachers gain experience and skill in collaboration through the PTLC, the quality of professional conversations substantially improves.

Professional Development That Impacts Classroom Practice

Change efforts that do little or nothing to affect what occurs in classrooms will have little or no effect on student achievement. A number of leading researchers (Fullan, 2007; Knapp, 2003; Richardson & Placier, 2001) propose that collaborative curriculum development and assessment of student work is a meaningful process that helps teachers improve practice.

All of this suggests that implementing the PTLC is a viable strategy for ongoing, job-embedded professional development and that districts and schools, operating as learning communities, need to make adult learning a prerequisite to student learning (Tobia, 2007).

Knapp (2003) identifies the following essential themes in professional development that are likely to deepen teachers' knowledge and skill *and* lead to application of this knowledge and skill in the classrooms:

- Challenging teachers intellectually with powerful images of teaching and learning.
- Engaging teachers as active learners and offering concrete images of what high-quality practice looks like while taking them more deeply into the content they are teaching and how learners acquire it.
- Reinforcing teacher learning over time through repeated and varied exposure to ideas and through interactions with colleagues, who can act as a resource.

- Offering teachers ways to address the specific problems they face, including the demands and pressures placed on them by state and local reform expectations.

Leadership for the Improvement of Teaching and Learning

District and school leaders are now called on to create conditions in which educational professionals work together toward common goals, learn and apply research-based practices, and improve teaching and learning.

Leaders are also called on to nurture collaboration within and between multiple levels of the system and ensure that professional learning, collegiality, respect, and trust become part of the system's culture (Bryk & Schneider, 2003; Tobia, 2007; Tschannen-Moran, 2004).

Although teachers ultimately determine what is learned at the classroom level, principals in high-performing schools help provide strong leadership and supportive conditions for learning (McEwan, 2003; National Association of Elementary School Principals, 2001). School leadership is central to conditions that support teacher learning (Barth, 2006; Cotton, 2003; Mitchell & Sackney, 2001).

Leaders must become champions of an improvement process that requires everyone to view themselves as leaders and learners. In so doing, the school as a whole develops as a learning organization—a culture where people see themselves connected to each other and the world, where creative thinking is nurtured, and "where people are continually learning how to learn together" (Senge, 1990, p. 3).

SUMMARY

Using the PTLC as a strategy for promoting alignment of the written, taught, and tested curriculum also provides a means to develop a PLC in a school. Adopting a systemic approach to this end within a district becomes even more powerful in ensuring more than isolated *pockets* of improvement. Acknowledging the interdependent nature of systemic improvement calls for concerted change at the district, school, and classroom levels and a sharper definition of leaders' roles at all levels of the system in ensuring effective instruction. Such changes, however, need to occur within a culture of collegiality, collaboration, and continuous improvement so that all classrooms in all schools within a district are bound together with a common goal: to ensure learning experiences of the highest order for all students.

7

+

Case Story Overview

Kristine Kiefer Hipp and Jane Bumpers Huffman

In order to delve more deeply into the dilemmas and challenges faced by leaders, it is useful to consider extended cases of practice. When used in professional preparation programs or inservice professional development, cases have the advantage of leading participants to grapple with a select number of authentic and significant educational problems.

—Murphy (1992, p. 152)

Fullan (1995, 2000) added that most school reform efforts have created overload and fragmentation, thereby resulting in a lack of coherence and meaning that continues to divert us from issues of greatest importance: teaching and learning. For instance, many governance structures have been designed to empower a greater number of staff in decision making, yet students fail to benefit. Efforts are often unrelated to curriculum and instructional issues, and systems are not aligned to focus on the process it takes to move students to higher levels of achievement (Fullan, 1995; Guskey & Peterson, 1993; Lindle, 1995/1996; Newmann & Wehlage, 1995).

In the guise of teacher empowerment, Brown (1995) states: "Traditional opportunities for teacher decision-making have done little to advance the professionalism of teachers, or to involve them in critical educational concerns" (p. 337).

The accounts of these school reform efforts come and go, often carrying rich details of their stories with them. So, how do schools move from implementing innovation to sustaining change? How do schools move from norms of isolation to norms of collaboration, inquiry, and community? How do schools grow into mature professional communities? How can school leaders become prepared to create communities that continuously learn to improve teaching and student performance?

The purpose of providing three case stories for analysis is based on practices we have observed as we work in schools to create PLCs. Hipp and Huffman and their research team studied the first two schools longitudinally for several years. Data from formal and informal assessments were used to craft these stories. In the third case study, Hipp served as an instructor and researcher through a federal Wallace Foundation grant to support the efforts of the primary author, the principal, over 1 ½ years. In this story the principal reflects on the challenges encountered during her 2-year tenure as principal.

The schools include PreK–8 schools in urban, suburban, and rural settings across three states and are at varying stages of PLC development. The stories illuminate different themes or characteristics associated with PLCs and give a good idea of how different PLCs develop and grow. These themes are noted in the following brief overview of each school and discussed more fully in the case stories.

School 1: Lake Elementary (PreK–8)

- Socioeconomic status: Low-middle income rural.
- PLC level: Sustaining; continuous growth over 12 years despite challenges.
- Themes: Plantation as a Learning Family; Undeviating Focus; Collaboration, Shared Responsibility, and Accountability; and Inclusive Leadership Fosters a Culture of Teaching and Learning.

School 2: Mineral Springs Middle School (6–8)

- Socioeconomic status: Low-income suburban.
- PLC level: Implementing; commitment to PLCs even through leadership changes.
- Themes: Leadership; Focus; Relationships; and Central Office.

School 3: Metcalfe School (K4–8)

- Socioeconomic status: Low-income urban.
- PLC level: Initiating; significant short-term change focused on developing communication and trusting relationships across the principal, staff, and parents to improve conditions for students to be successful.
- Themes: Strong and Passionate Principal Leadership; Dedicated Staff, High Expectations, and Professional Development; Positive

Climate and Culture Focused on Student Achievement; and External Support Systems.

Each story includes the following sections:

- Introduction: Provides an introduction to each case story by profiling school demographics and identifying major issues.
- Principal's Initial Reflections (Case Study 3 only): Includes perceptions of the current situation and necessary steps to address the enormity of the challenges in reshaping the school culture, teacher morale, and student achievement within the short two years the principal served.
- The Story: Describes the three case stories and the explanation of contextual factors.
- Meeting the Challenge: Explains what was done in each of the schools to address the major issues.
- Analyzing Practices: Offers readers the opportunity to apply strategies related to the PLC dimensions and other factors. It includes tools to establish and redirect reform and other factors in relation to the case story and the reader's school.

The general purpose of these stories is to allow participants to analyze information presented and generate further questions and areas of interest in need of study. We purposefully include a mature PLC, which despite unpredictable and significant challenges, maintains practices that sustain the school's PLC efforts; a PLC that has experienced the ups and downs associated with leadership changes, but persisted in its development efforts; and a school not meeting adequate yearly progress (AYP),

Table 7.1 Demographics for Case Story Schools (2007–2008)

Schools	Number of Students	Number of Instructional Staff	Student Ethnicity (%)	Limited English Proficiency (%)	Economically Dis-advantaged (%)	Student Attendance (%)
Lake	1,038	74	97.9 White; 2.1 Other	0	30	95.8
Mineral Springs	1,007	80	86.6 Hispanic; 7.7 African American; 5.7 White	11.1	75.1	96.3
Metcalfe	335	23	99 African American	0	95	89.4

but through the expertise of a new principal, the school community is changing after only two short years.

We hope readers will challenge each other's thinking with these authentic stories, which reflect multiple and confounding issues. Our primary goal in presenting these case stories is to stimulate inquiry among school administrators and staff, as well as faculty and students in educational leadership programs. Moreover, we urge educators to generate their own perspectives, identify related issues and problems, and develop potential solutions or next steps for their own school story.

8

Case Story #1

Lake Elementary (PreK–8)

Dianne F. Olivier and Kristine Kiefer Hipp

INTRODUCTION

Lake Elementary is located in a southwestern, rural school district composed of 21 schools and approximately 15,000 students. This PreK–8 school enrolls 1,059 students comprised of 99 percent White and 1 percent African American. 30 percent of the students qualify for free or reduced lunch and there are no students classified as limited English proficient.

Besides a principal of 5 years, Lake has two assistant principals, three guidance counselors, 75 teachers, and nine paraprofessionals.

The school's 2007–2008 mission statement reads "Lake Elementary Community will provide the highest quality of teaching and learning for all students to raise achievement and to ensure life long learners and productive citizens." The school improvement plan for this year focuses on scientifically based research strategies including meaningful engaged learning and data-driven decision making targeting school-wide behavior and differentiated instruction to meet the needs of all learners.

The district's underlying theme of educational excellence has withstood the test of time at Lake. High student achievement is reflected in student performance on state-mandated assessments. The school previously received recognition reflecting growth and performance and continues to demonstrate annual improvement including meeting AYP in all subgroup populations.

The author researchers have studied the transitions that have occurred at Lake for almost 10 years. Interactions have occurred through on-site visits and data collection including surveys, interviews, and document reviews maintaining up-to-date information regarding Lake as a PLC. Midway through our study the following impressions emerged and provide a glimpse of how the school functions:

- Lake is a "learning family" committed to staff and student learning.
- The staff is united by an undeviating focus on student learning.
- Data-driven decisions lead to collaboration, shared responsibility, and accountability among stakeholders.
- Inclusive leadership fosters a culture that strives for high-quality teaching and learning.

The uniqueness of this school's continuous progress enticed the researchers to monitor and deepen our understanding as to how Lake's staff was able to sustain their improvement efforts year after year. The accountability process can be perceived as penalizing schools at higher levels because their potential for growth is limited, thereby the process as "lived out" can be seen as demeaning and can eradicate motivation in our children's educators.

So how do high performing schools, like Lake Elementary, continue to challenge both teachers and students to beat the odds?

THE STORY

Lake as a Learning Family

"When you walk down the hall, you hear learning going on."

The reputation of Lake Elementary as a family was reinforced by the response of staff and community to the fallout from Hurricane Katrina in the fall of 2005. The aftermath of this disastrous storm affected many areas beyond the southeastern United States, including schools like Lake located in the Southwest.

During the weeks following the storm, approximately 80 displaced students were welcomed into Lake. The staff warmly opened their arms, their hearts, and their classrooms to those students and families who were driven from their homes and schools. In addition to the influx of students, Lake also served as a haven for three displaced teachers.

An unexpected and immediate increase in student population can be cause for concern; however, this school readily accepted the challenge according to the principal:

It was pretty amazing to watch it happen . . . the teaching community and community in general, everybody made them feel welcomed. What our teachers did with those three ladies was unbelievable. They [displaced teachers] didn't want to leave when it was time for them to go. Our teachers just brought them in, made them feel comfortable, and made them feel like part of the family first and then they were there for them everyday . . . helping them with lesson plans, helping them with assessment, just guiding them. They were there holding there hands every step of the way.

Although the response for others in time of need is remarkable, the sense of a learning family is reinforced throughout the school and is indeed the norm. This family culture is observed throughout the school as teachers share comments reflecting genuine interest and underlying care for their colleagues and students. They share a feeling of security in relating to each other whether it's on a personal level or discussing classroom practices. "We bounce ideas off of each other . . . constantly go to each other." It is understood among teachers that all teachers at Lake "care about kids . . . and what is best for our students."

There are strong connections among teachers and between teachers and students resulting in strong interactions. Caring relationships exist among staff and students, and these relationships are the result of high levels of trust and respect.

The essence of Lake as a learning family and the strong level of commitment are readily observed inside and outside the school campus. One teacher stated it succinctly, "Once you get in the school, you don't leave," as teachers are vying throughout the district to "land a job at Lake."

Teachers have a voice and are treated as professionals empowered in their own learning. Professional staff members at Lake and community residents view this school as having an excellent reputation within the local community, the entire school district, and beyond.

One teacher explained, "There are always teachers waiting to get into Lake. There is a feeling of security from the support you get from the teachers . . . the positive atmosphere . . . let's get to work."

Teachers have noted the role of professional learning at Lake. Said one, "We search for new ideas and hopefully our learning will filter down to the students, but that's going to take time." Another commented, "It's amazing to watch how much people can learn just feeding off of each other." Another acknowledged the teachers' primary focus, "We always think of students first."

School staff and parents described Lake as "a tight community" reflecting family values. "Teachers model togetherness at Lake" and "trust is building; it doesn't happen overnight." "Trust is work, but we are alike in work ethics, values, purpose, and philosophy. It takes time."

Relationships were revealed to be not only strong inside, but "outside the walls of the school" as well. There was a sense of community as a very close-knit family. The intense level of commitment to be the best is evident from this comment: "Here everybody works so hard because the teachers . . . want to excel. . . . We want a good school and everybody's willing to share everything they have, so it makes it even better."

Undeviating Focus

"Keep learning—the focus is on children no matter what the challenge."

Even in the early years of establishing a PLC, challenges were often perceived as opportunities:

Our administration is very creative, getting around obstacles in ways that benefit students. If it's something that we really feel is going to benefit our students and we really want to do this, even though it may (not) be quite in line with what we are allowed to do, we're very innovative in coming up with things.

When teachers are passionate about a common belief, they collectively feel they can achieve anything.

I think we stumbled across a little catch phrase, "We believe" and that pretty much says it in a nutshell. We believe and you can put the three dots behind it. We believe in our students . . . we believe in our school . . . we believe our students can learn . . . we believe they have the right to learn . . . we believe we have the right to teach. We believe in everything . . . we believe that anything is possible.

In time, teachers re-evaluated their roles and found they served students more as "facilitators" and prided themselves in being good role models . . . being enthusiastic learners themselves for students to mirror. "Kids see that. In turn, we guide them to be advocates for their own learning."

This undeviating focus on student learning has been strengthened in the past few years as dramatic changes in student population caused teachers to enhance teaching and learning strategies in order to meet new challenges.

The student population has recently changed from the previous small percentages of students qualifying for either special education services or free and reduced lunch. Within the last 3 years the number of students eligible for free and reduced lunch has risen. There also has been a considerable rise in identification of students needing learning modifications and accommodations, a dramatic increase (70 to 225 students) in Affidavit students (indicating those living on someone else's property or with multiple families), and a significant increase in special education students.

The changing demographics resulted in the hiring of three additional special education teachers and the necessity to expand and enhance teaching strategies. This shift initially resulted in the need to "focus on academic deficits of these students . . . what we need to do and how do we need to go there."

Although conversations centered on meeting the needs of these newly identified learners with special needs, teachers were also facing new mandated requirements related to implementation of comprehensive curricula, benchmarks, content standards, grade-level expectations, and a wide range of assessments. This transition in student needs required a shift in teacher mentality, especially for teachers who previously had few if any special needs students.

The administration focused on providing all teachers with the necessary resources. Skilled personnel with expertise from outside and within the school worked closely with teachers in their classrooms to differentiate their teaching strategies in order to address the varying differences among learners.

By steadily moving forward, positive results were observed. As noted by one classroom teacher, "it's starting to make sense now; I cannot keep doing the same things I used to do."

Teachers' conversations about student learning now incorporate "talk about specific children and what they need . . . determining who needs what . . . how the class or group functions as a whole . . . taking into account different types of students and styles of learners . . . differentiation of instruction."

Although teachers felt confident in their level of communication, the shift in student population and greater diversity in learner needs has enriched the dialogue about student achievement during teaming time, according to one teacher:

> We talk about our students' progress and if they are making progress . . . what are some different strategies that we might use to help them make progress . . . if there's a skill that I just can't get across to my students, I'll walk across the hall and ask my coworker if she has a better way of getting that point across to the students. We're always thinking about different strategies, different levels of students, different ways of learning, and different ways to incorporate that into our lessons.

The focus on student learning at all levels has resulted in the implementation of many new strategies and increased opportunities for teaching and learning.

New comprehensive and challenging curricula have been implemented across the school in all core content areas. New reading strategies have been linked to the differentiation of instruction. Intensity of interventions has been increased by incorporating at an early stage and implementing over a longer period of time. Reading interventions are provided for all students with additional focus on small groups of at-risk students.

To address the needs of all learners, Lake has developed programs to provide for those students not qualifying for state supplemental services. To assist students who might fall through the cracks, enrichment classes are offered for academic reinforcement targeting the average or mid-level students.

For the higher performing students, the Saturday Lake Academy was implemented with emphasis on higher order thinking skills, logical thinking activities, and "lots of interaction among teachers and students." The Academy is seen as serving a significant role in the substantial increase of students performing at *advanced* levels on state-mandated tests over the last few years.

The incorporation of new and innovative strategies has "made a difference with test results . . . fewer students scoring below the required minimum than expected."

The implementation of new strategies and programs and enhancement of those techniques that are working reinforce the staff's commitment to a shared vision for school improvement with an undeviating focus on student learning. It is indeed obvious that the policies and programs embraced by Lake are aligned to their school vision.

Collaboration, Shared Responsibility, and Accountability

"Everybody's working together, like pieces of a puzzle. We put the pieces together and that's why it works!"

At Lake Elementary school improvement planning maintains the focus of instructional effectiveness and student learning. All played a part in the vision; the intent was to distribute accountability to everyone as partners. Lake went to great lengths to get the entire school community involved, "We got the word out to parents and even hired babysitters to get people here." This process set the stage for staff to be empowered.

The vision has given them the power to express themselves and to realistically make changes.

Lake involves the entire community. "By working together we garner resources for kids that we would otherwise do without." The school has an excellent local reputation and has established multiple connections and community partners.

The Lake School staff acknowledge they have exceptionally strong ties with parents. "There is a strong parental presence on campus and at home. Parents are here daily and are ready on the spot. They let teachers teach!"

Over the last few years, the previous two parent organizations have merged into one enhanced group, Reaching Out and Reconnecting (ROAR). This new organization serves as a parent-teacher group, with the parents and teachers working hand-in-hand to continue to move the school forward. Communication is regularly maintained. Parents want information and are notified about most everything, especially student progress and tests.

The parent group supports classroom needs by actively participating in fundraising, after-school tutoring, and advocating our needs in the community. This past year the ROAR organization hosted a Blue Ribbon Bizarre to celebrate the achievements of the school. The turnout from the school and community was remarkable and the parent volunteers raised $20,000 to benefit Lake.

Additionally, parents substitute at the end of the day for primary teachers who meet in learning teams called Critical Friends to discuss student work and resolve school and classroom issues in large cross-grade and subject level teams.

Collaboration is a key ingredient to the success of teachers and students at Lake. Teachers work with each other through daily grade-level meetings. Teachers routinely set aside time to share issues and plan. "We . . . find out what's going on in someone else's classroom . . . how you can connect your lesson across the curriculum." Lake teachers do not adhere to the norm of isolation; instead, teachers readily express their feelings of uniqueness. "We have an openness to share . . . anything . . . from art projects to a change in the curriculum. . . . No one hides their ideas, instead, it's . . . I had this great idea, I want you to try it with your kids."

The willingness to assist each other set the stage for a strong sense of responsibility among teachers to share their personal practices. The teachers easily recognize that this attitude of *what's mine is ours* is not the standard at most schools. "I've been at another school where your project, your special thing that you've discovered is your thing and I'm not going to share it because it's mine and I don't want you to do it better than me, so I won't tell you about it."

There is an overwhelming sense that mutual sharing is very productive and best for all—teachers and students. "You don't feel . . . that you're giving it and you're carrying their weight . . . you're sharing because you know . . . in turn . . . they're giving you something." Sharing is viewed as "non-competitive . . . we share ideas . . . take care of each other."

Collaboration and shared responsibility are also observed through the integration of two new teacher coaches, one at the primary level and one working with the middle grade teachers. The teacher coaches are recognized as exceptional or master teachers and work directly with teachers within their classrooms. The focal point with the teacher coach is the integration and refinement of new strategies, provision of resources, and overall assistance in the teaching and learning process.

The teacher coach concept has been embraced by the staff, "I think they're wonderful, they answer all of your questions . . . they really help you."

Although the teacher coach program serves as another tool, the staff at Lake have learned to rely on each other for overall support and the strength of collegial support is appreciated.

> I was at another school and as a new teacher here . . . everyone here is so welcoming and helpful. I consider myself lucky to get in here [Lake] . . . the level of support . . . when they ask you to do something, they show you how to do it . . . they're not like some schools that tell you to just do it, to deal with it, do it yourself.

The staff are continuously involved in discussing and making decisions about school issues. Data-driven decisions serve as the focal point for change. The staff feel more comfortable and confident in making their own decisions according to what is best for their students, rather than merely following the lead of other schools or teachers.

Teachers express pride in the fact that they consider their role and their school as a bit of a rebel, as indicated in the following remarks:

> If we really don't like what Central Office has told us, we just quietly do something different until we can prove that it works better than what they told us to do . . . and we've done that on many different occasions. If we're told that certain practices will no longer be utilized, but we feel strongly about them, then we'll bring you the data to prove that it works . . . it's surprisingly easy to find out what works on our kids.

An example was offered relating to a supplemental language program that was no longer considered part of the district English language program. Teachers at Lake were able to share specific data with central office personnel indicating the success of their students with the specific language strategies. With the data in hand to support their cause, district personnel agreed with the teachers that these strategies should remain an integral part of their language program.

Collaboration and sharing responsibility can be observed through the mentoring program for new teachers, as well as shared accountability for hiring of new teachers.

New teachers to Lake are assigned a mentor from among the teaching staff. Parent volunteers substitute for the mentors to allow them to spend time with the new teachers within their classrooms. The mentors possess a "coach mentality," and they provide ongoing assistance to their colleagues. As one new teacher expressed, "coming on board I definitely felt that I was able to get the support needed . . . very welcoming."

Lake has a history of a very stable teaching force. However, when a teaching slot opens up, the hiring process goes beyond the administration with teachers actively participating in the hiring process.

The principal indicated that significant interest occurs when a teaching position becomes available, as the school receives 100 to 150 applications each year from new and experienced teachers. However, the dedication, interest, and concern among staff members provide for an effective process. He said,

> [i]n selecting teachers . . . everybody is involved . . . if it's a second grade teacher, then we have a team of second grade teachers . . . they all meet . . . they are going to be working with them . . . they're in the trenches with them . . . [our] teachers have such a sense of commitment, when they have input in selecting teachers, they want to be sure those teachers are the most effective.

Inclusive Leadership Fosters a Culture of Teaching and Learning

> "Teachers are leaders; whereas the administration is the backbone of the school."

Leadership permeates throughout the school at different levels. As one teacher leader described, "It's like an onion; it's in layers, because we have so many different people heading up different areas. Our leadership team is made up of teachers who have been trained in facilitation. They come from all different levels and curriculum disciplines."

Such preparation reflected a "grow your own" leadership, "We see new faces taking on leadership roles." Teachers at Lake feel very comfortable sharing leadership and responsibility as reflected by one teacher:

> We can go to the administrator's office and suggest that we do something. . . . Its very comforting to know that you can share your ideas and that you have input into what's going to happen in the whole school, not just your classroom . . . classroom behavior, discipline, extra-curricula ideas, reading and math programs, promoting interests.

Teachers and assistant principals take the lead in issues around curriculum and instruction. Teachers have the freedom to do what they think is best for students. "They don't tell me how to teach. I can change what needs to be changed to benefit students, to be fair to students."

The principal voiced confidence in his teachers, "I'm blessed with the overall competence of my faculty. Our teachers also model good instruction. I have many teachers who are leaders, but it's about leading by example."

The teachers feel support in their shared vision. One teacher explained, "Our principal's focus is on student achievement and [he] is receptive to suggestions and input from teachers." Another said, "Administration is very supportive. . . . I live outside of the district and I pass two other district elementary schools to get here. . . . This is where I want to be."

At first, several teachers viewed shared leadership as administrators abdicating responsibility; now they view facilitation as just a part of a collaborative effort. This is not to say the principal divorces himself from teaching and learning; rather, "He is visible in every classroom; everybody sees him everyday."

Other teachers indicate the administrators are responsive but also "keep order in the school and make sure it's safe and hold everyone accountable."

This form of leadership marks the manner in which decisions are made, responsibilities are assumed, and trust develops. Whereas teachers take the lead around issues of teaching and learning, the principal focuses on strategies and resources to support their work and creativity. "I think our administrators trust their teachers with their ideas and what they think about their students because, after all, we know our students. And they trust us and it's mutual."

Lake's school culture influences the effectiveness of the school and guides the operations on a daily basis. The culture forces attention on those issues that are deemed truly important to making the school successful for all.

The school maintains many unique structures, committees, and learning activities that target *all* student needs including an array of programs, such as Critical Friends, peer-coaching and critique, learning styles, multiple reading programs/strategies, Early Literacy, at-risk and exceptional educational needs programs, looping at primary levels, positive behavior support programs, enrichment activities, and common planning time.

In this strong culture, professional development is embedded in this school; it is visible in the hallways, the teachers' lounge, after school in tutoring sessions, and through daily team meetings. When teachers attend conferences, they share what they learned with others. The focus of conversation is on learning and the curriculum. "Vertical and horizontal meetings [also] keep us on the same page. People even take notes for those who can't attend."

In addition to Critical Friends, a staff member said, "A big step is the coaching and relying on peers, having someone to turn to for help and sharing that—I want to call it teaching wisdom—and it's not only with veteran, but new teachers have a lot to share too."

Early seeds had been planted for sharing personal practice with reservation, for example, video-taping lessons as a means for self and peer critique, albeit using a non-threatening rubric; few took the risk outside of a select group of peers. These concepts are now reinforced through the strength of the Teacher Coach program.

Critical Friends has been credited widely for the dramatic change in the way teachers came together as a faculty to learn through sharing and feedback. Teachers across grade and content levels meet to address critical issues, classroom dilemmas, and student work. These teachers represent a "wide range of personalities and views." The facilitators of each Critical Friends team shared issues and identify common student needs in an effort to bring the whole school together. This process has "built relationships and fostered trust . . . we've become valuable resources to one another."

MEETING THE CHALLENGE

Regardless of their reputation as a high-performing school, Lake faces challenges like any other school. The most significant change is one of sustainability: how to maintain effective practices and programs, high achieving students in light of shifting demographics, unexpected disasters, and day-to-day dilemmas.

No Child Left Behind mandates continuous school improvement for the school as a whole, as well as the necessity to meet AYP for all subgroup populations. Lake Elementary remains one of the top-performing schools in their district, despite changes in student demographics reflected in the increase of at-risk students and those identified with learning disabilities.

The staff at Lake has worked hard to maintain the high level of motivation amid accountability demands. Evidence of their constant push for learning for students and teachers is seen in the success of achieving AYP for all subgroup populations, including the increasing number of at-risk and special education students, as well as the steady progress in their school performance score.

The principal expressed the difficulty in maintaining a forward movement when you are at the top, "it gets harder and harder to continue to move forward . . . but we must be proactive . . . our population has changed dramatically . . . we've held our own . . . teachers are aware of the necessity to change their teaching styles. . . . We're doing everything we can as our population has changed . . . as a three-star school, we are still in the top in the district."

A recurring challenge is to address diverse student needs with the increasing population of at-risk, Section 504, and special education students. This challenge is indeed a focus as evidenced by their yearly school improvement plan that centers on providing meaningful engaged learning and differentiation of instruction to meet the needs of all learners. It will be essential for teachers to enhance their work across grade and content levels, developing a strong foundation to expand the skills of the changing population. Lake staff must continue to routinely engage in dialogue that reflects the need for continued inquiry and improvement.

In reflecting on strengths of Lake, the family concept was repeatedly recognized, "Working together . . . we all work together . . . we are a big family here. . . . Everybody who's stepped foot on this campus and spent the day or part of the day comes away with that feeling. . . . They know why the kids care, they know why the teachers care, it's because of how everyone's treated here."

The central focus on student achievement that Lake has demonstrated over the years will continue to serve the teachers and the students. The staff will persist in their conversations about teaching and learning and will continue to do everything possible for student success because it's the right thing to do.

As one experienced teacher concluded, "Yes, we take our jobs personally—it makes us do a better job."

ANALYZING PROFESSIONAL
LEARNING COMMUNITY PRACTICES

1. Generate evidence related to the following PLC dimensions:

   - Shared and supportive leadership

     - How was leadership capacity created, shared, and implemented?

   - Shared values and vision

     - How were the school's efforts aligned to the school's vision, values, and goals?

   - Collective learning and application

     - How was the staff involved in focused and meaningful learning?

   - Shared personal practice

     - How did teachers share their practice?

   - Supportive conditions—structures

     - How were structures that support the culture of the PLC established?

- Supportive conditions—relationships

  - How were relationships of trust and respect established?

- External factors

  - To what degree was the entire school community engaged?

2. Generate evidence related to additional strategies and critical factors:

   - What evidence demonstrates a focus on student learning?
   - Provide examples that illustrate a culture of high-quality teaching and learning.
   - Provide examples of collaboration.
   - What evidence indicates the level of leadership capacity?
   - Provide evidence of the level of collective efficacy.
   - Discuss this case story and the relationship to sustainability.
   - What evidence of external factors (e.g., central office personnel, parents, and community members) or resources support the school as a PLC?

3. Compare this case story to your own school(s). Consider the PLC dimensions, additional strategies, and critical factors.

4. Apply any relevant tools to your own school(s):

   - The PLCO.
   - The PLC-ICM.
   - The ESS-ICM.
   - The PLCDR.
   - The Initial PLC Plan.

9

Case Story #2

Mineral Springs Middle School (6–8)

Anita M. Pankake and Jane Bumpers Huffman

INTRODUCTION

Mineral Springs Middle School (MSMS) is located in a highly industrialized area near a city in the southwest. The parent community includes primarily first-generation immigrants who look to the school to provide the American dream for their children.

Based on the 2000 census, the community of Mineral Springs has a population of approximately 10,500. The racial makeup of the city population was 22.2 percent White, 7.5 percent African American, 69.5 percent Hispanic, and 0.8 percent other. The median household income in the community was $31,660 with nearly one-quarter of the population below the poverty line.

The school district, Mineral Springs Independent School District (MSISD), includes the community of Mineral Springs and segments of land within the large city of which Mineral Springs is a suburb.

In 2003, MSISD reported a student enrollment of 20,000 housed at 22 campuses (3 high schools, 4 middle schools, 13 elementary schools, a sixth grade campus, and an educational center). Currently, the district claims a student population of 21,180 attending classes at 23 campuses.

The MSISD mission is to prepare students to become productive citizens and lifelong learners.

Based on the state's rating system, MSISD was labeled as Exemplary in 2002, Recognized in 2004, and Academically Acceptable every year since. No ratings were issued to districts or schools during the 2003 school year because of a change in the state's testing. That year was used to recalculate the various inputs used for the ratings, including the new tests. Additionally, since the 2003 school year, state-mandated tests in the areas of social studies and science are now included in the calculations of ratings for both districts and schools.

MSMS's mission reflects that of the district, "making students successful lifelong learners."

MSMS serves students in grades 6, 7, and 8; it has seen a slight decrease in the student population since 2003, now enrolling slightly more than 900 students. Seventy-nine teachers, one principal, three assistant principals, three counselors, one librarian, and eight instructional specialists currently serve MSMS. These numbers indicate a reduction of three full-time employees since 2003 that aligns with the enrollment decreases resulting from the addition of a fifth middle school to the district.

For the 2001–2002 academic year, MSMS was rated Recognized by the state and had an attendance rate of 96.3 percent. Between 2002 and 2006, the school earned an Academically Acceptable rating until the 2006–2007 school year when the rating returned to Recognized.

The ethnic breakdown of the student population has changed slightly over the past 4 years. The percentage of African American students has dropped from 7.7 to 5.2. Hispanic students now make up 89.4 percent of the enrollments, up from 86.6 percent in 2003, with the percentage of white students remaining relatively steady with 5.7 percent in 2003 and 5.2 percent in 2006–2007. However, the percent of limited English proficient population has nearly doubled from 11.1 to 20.8 percent.

The school remains a school-wide Title I campus. The economically disadvantaged percentage as determined by free and reduced lunch numbers was 75.1 percent in 2003 but increased to 85.7 percent during the 2006–2007 school year. The per pupil expenditure amount was $6,186, which has increased very little during this time, rising to $6,302 for 2006–2007.

The percentage of students meeting the state standard on the state-mandated tests increased each year from 1996 through 2001. Table 9.1 displays the percentage of students meeting the standard in each of the subject areas tested.

Although percentage of students meeting state-mandated standards has varied slightly, the rating for the school, as a whole, moved from Academically Acceptable in 1999 to Recognized in 2000 and remained so through 2002. In 2003, the state changed their standardized tests; because of this, no state ratings for districts or schools were issued that year. Table 9.2 displays MSMS's performance on the new test beginning in 2004.

Table 9.1 Mineral Springs Middle School: TAAS Test Scores and State Ratings

	1996 Accept-able	1997 Accept-able	1998 Accept-able	1999 Rec-ognized	2000 Rec-ognized	2001 Rec-ognized	2002 Rec-ognized
Reading (%)	62.5	79.6	78.9	87.8	86.3	89.8	89.4
Writing (%)	64.0	76.3	75.0	92	91.6	89.7	91.9
Math (%)	57.1	72.5	80.8	90.9	93.1	96.3	95
Social Studies (%)	—	—	—	—	—	68.9	87.3
All Tests (%)	47.3	64.1	70.4	83.5	83.5	86.8	85.9

Table 9.2 Mineral Springs Middle School: TAKS Test Scores and State Ratings*

	2002–03 No rating—first year of new test	2003–04 Academically Acceptable	2004–05 Academically Acceptable	2005–06 Academically Acceptable	2006–07 Recognized
Reading (%)	74.8	81	73	76	83
Writing (%)	77.8	89	85	89	92
Math (%)	52.0	63	59	66	75
Social Studies (%)	76.1	86	85	71	81
Science (%)	—	—	—	35	42

*Mineral Springs Middle School met standard (sum of all grades tested).

THE STORY

Much of the literature regarding PLCs offers readers a snapshot of a school or district at a particular point in time. This case, however, presents information about the development and implementation of a PLC over nearly a decade.

The long-term view allows the reader to see that the overall direction of development is improvement; on the other hand, it also permits a glimpse at the points when some regression occurs as the journey unfolds. Additionally, this case demonstrates the powerful influence that can be exercised at the district level on PLC development at a particular campus.

As you read the MSMS story, watch for information that will help you address the following questions:

- What seems to cause the interruptions in continuous improvement in the school?

- What actions were taken to redirect the process?
- How might the development at MSMS been different if the district context had not been so supportive?

The researchers have studied transitions at MSMS for 7 years. Initially, after the PLC training for the 1998 SEDL study, the researchers visited MSMS to conduct surveys, group and individual interviews, and to review documents. MSMS staff also received training in the PLC process from the authors and from their principal and assistant principal.

The researchers returned to the district two additional times to interview various MSMS administration and staff; during the last visit completed in 2005, interviews were also conducted with central office administrators, as well as campus personnel. Based on the transcripts from initial research at MSMS, four themes were identified as prevalent in the school culture: leadership, focus, relationships, and the involvement of central office administrators. The 2005 interview transcripts were examined for evidence of the continuation of these themes.

We tell the story of MSMS as a PLC regarding these four themes over several years, by moving back and forth between 1998 and 2005. The four themes were developing simultaneously, although some moved slower than others. There are also some points at which the development is stalled or even set back; we see this as crucial in describing the situation realistically.

Leadership

"We make decisions together." (2003)
"It's not somebody in the administration building that's go[ing] to decide for you, it's your leadership committee here that's going to."(2005)

In 2003, recognizing that leadership is shared at many levels and in various ways, support can be found in the following statement by an assistant principal: "The team leaders and department chairs are quasi-administrators. They are in charge of academics, grades and disciplining the students." The librarian also commented about teacher leaders: "Teachers have good ideas and aren't hesitant to speak up. They provide suggestions, make decisions, ask other's opinions and adjust accordingly." In 2005, individuals interviewed continued to identify leadership in the school as shared at a variety of levels. One of the department chairs at MSMS talked about ways in which leadership in the school is exercised:

We have a leadership team that is made up of department chairs. I think a lot of decisions are made in there. The principal and the assistant principals are also meeting in there. . . . We are scheduled to meet once a month. . . . Our faculty meetings are exactly the same way. So, it's once a month . . . team leaders are on there too . . . Department chairs and team leaders.

To emphasize the seriousness with which the district seeks teachers as leaders, the process for identifying a new principal for the school was described by the department chair for social studies:

> We're going to get a new principal . . . so we met with the teaching staff at the administration building last week . . . we were given a questionnaire and so each teacher is giving their [perspective], you know what qualities are you looking for in a new principal, so they have a say so in what they are looking for and then they're [District Chief of Staff and the Human Resources Director] coming out Thursday . . . so he kind of said ok. It's not somebody in the administration building that's go[ing] to decide for you, it's your leadership committee here that's going to.

Leadership succession appears to have been important in sustaining this school culture. The principal in 2003 (Mrs. C) was previously an assistant principal at MSMS. In 2003 she had been the principal for 3 years; by the 2005 academic year, she was ready to retire after serving 9 years at the school in one capacity or another. The principal before 2003 (Mrs. H) had moved to an administrative position at central office in 2003. Prior to assuming the principalship at MSMS, she had served as an assistant principal for the school. Additionally, a former lead teacher who had moved to the assistant principal position in 2003 had moved to central office to work with his former principal (Mrs. H) in the special programs division by the time the 2005 interviews occurred.

The leadership succession here, at the school, and elsewhere in the district seems to have played a significant role in sustaining efforts to function as a PLC by keeping a level of stability in vision and mission, leadership style, and focus on student learning.

Two succession issues were of primary concern on the district's 2005 agenda. First, the new superintendent was making his leadership style and substance known to the school community. He was an experienced superintendent, but new to this district. The previous superintendent had been a teacher, campus principal, and central office administrator in the district prior to assuming the superintendency. Her tenure in that position was from 1995 through 2004.

The new superintendent began work in the 2004–2005 academic year, and with his tenure came various changes in leadership at the central office and the schools. A new position at central office, Chief of Staff, was created for and assumed by an individual from outside the district. He commented on the strategy used in making this succession work:

Now, [the new superintendent] came in and observed the district for one year, then brought me in mid-year, in January. Told me to help him look at the district for 6 more months and then continue to build the continuous improvement model. We reorganized and didn't bring any new people in at the top.

One of the assistant principals described these changes in leadership as disruptive to "everything." As is often the case in the early stages of change, issues and situations can be viewed quite differently depending on where you are in the organization. After nine years of having the same superintendent, adjusting to a new person resulted in additional changes in both personnel and practices throughout the district, including the exit of some central office administrators and the initiation of a new district-wide reading program.

The second leadership succession issue dealt with the 2005 retirement of the MSMS principal (Mrs. C) and the search for her replacement. Based on information shared by those interviewed in 2005, MSMS teachers were to play a direct role in the selection of the new principal. Several of the teachers would be chosen to serve on the search committee, and all of the teachers were given an opportunity to offer their ideas and opinions on a profile for this new leader. This was done through a site visit by the superintendent's chief of staff and the human resources director to hear what the teachers had to say. Additionally a written survey was used to gather information from everyone about preferred characteristics for the new leader. This process provided teachers with a strong voice in selecting the new leader for their school.

Focus

"The focus is to educate our students and to help them become productive citizens."(2003)
"[O]ur teachers are constantly looking for different ways to teach students; that's why we have them meet every other day." (2005)

In 1998, the principal (Mrs. H) commented on the perspective that she held for her staff and her staff for her. She reported: "What we want to do is we're a team, we're a family, but we have a job to do." She referenced the efforts underway to assist all of the teachers and administrators in helping all of the students. For example, physical education teachers and art teachers were helping with reading; principal and assistant principals were going to classrooms to help with teaching math.

At the time, MSMS focused on trying to regain recognized status and get 80 percent of students reading at a high level. The lead teacher in 1998 stated: "The goal is to produce a lifelong commitment to learning, success in both academic, technological and other fields. . . . Basically every decision that we make focuses on student learning."

Clearly, from 1998 to 2003, the principal and the team leaders were focused on how they could help the teachers reach the student learning goal. In 2003, the new principal (Mrs. C) identified students as the focus of the school. Similar to her predecessor, she stated her priority was students; she noted that it was "students first" with the previous principal and "students first" with her as well. She even indicated that the staff knew better than to bother her with something if it did not focus on or help the kids.

Teachers were interviewed by the researchers on site in spring of 2000. The teachers' comments verified that student achievement was the school focus and that expectations for both the teachers and the students had changed over time. One teacher noted that in years past it would not have been "a big deal" regarding what percentage of the kids did well on the state test. However, she noted in 2000: "We want to do well on the TAAS test every year. That's kind of like the main goal that everybody is aiming at right now."

In 2003, interviews with teachers individually and in focus groups garnered the following responses to the question, "What is most important in your school?"

- "Our students are first priority."
- "We're interested in our students' learning."
- "Learners, everything we do is learner-centered."
- "[The principal] makes it clear that we are here for the kids."
- "Creating successful students."

When asked about the monitoring of the school improvement process, an assistant principal commented that each department chair was responsible for going back through the action plan, checking on whether various tasks in the plan were completed, and if not, determining if the tasks should be modified, deleted, or postponed until the next year. The principal (Mrs. C) then added that this process continued throughout the year, "We have a little binder in the teacher's planning room that they actually go through and they look at the action plan constantly." She was quick to agree with one of the researchers that the school's action plan could be described as a living document that was used to guide the work of teachers and administrators in the school throughout the school year.

In the 2005 interviews, we probed for information on how that school and district developed the process that made them so successful over the decade. The Total Quality benchmarking tool was used to determine what practices were being implemented in other districts that might also be employed in MSMS. According to one of the central office administrators instrumental in initiating the process:

We looked at [other districts] . . . and looked at what they were doing in terms of aligning their curriculum; we developed what we call instructional focus activities. One of the problems that we identified up front and principals helped us to do this, was by the time we're getting to the test, kids haven't been exposed to everything that's on the test. We haven't taught everything and so they are being tested over things, over concepts they've never been taught. And so, what we did is we developed those instructional focus activities for every teacher . . . every day at the beginning of each content period, [the teacher teaches a] 10- to 15-minute instructional focus activity. It's correlated to the scope and sequence. It's actually easier to do now, because the TEKS[1] are more correlated to the test than the essential elements were.

At MSMS, the focus on students as a priority appears to have begun in 1998 when Mrs. H became principal, perhaps before, but certainly when she assumed the position. Throughout 1998 to 2003, the mantra regarding the school's focus remained the same. The depth and breadth of its adoption increased throughout the years, so that by 2003 it was not an administrative platitude, but rather a genuinely believed value that was reflected by staff behavior and embedded in the school culture. In 2005, this message was echoed by a MSMS assistant principal:

[O]ur teachers are constantly looking for different ways to teach students; that's why we have them meet every other day. All the grade level subject teachers meet and they're discussing . . . different ways of teaching what they're on . . . making sure every one is teaching the same thing. And, they have a chance to share what, how they are doing it or what activities they are using to get the point across . . . or what enrichment activity or your teaching styles for that child.

A teacher in the math department reinforced alignment with the focus on student learning when she was asked what she would put on her wish list for the school. Her response indicated her own feelings and also how she perceived the feelings of some of her colleagues:

That all teachers . . . want to be here and want to teach; that's their number one goal. That all kids learn. And I can't speak about all departments . . . I'm just thinking about the Math department *(laughter)*. Some come for the money: it's a job . . . some come because they love to teach and they don't care about the money.

A focus on student learning pervaded the district, as well as the school. A central office administrator commented:

[S]aying every child can learn is like saying every child can breathe. You can't stop them from learning. . . . It's not a question [of] whether they learn or don't learn. They're going to learn one way or another. . . . Question is, are they going to learn what you're supposed to be teaching them?

Relationships

"We have our own jobs and we support each other." (2003)
"You can't just go into your classroom . . . you can't say . . . gee, I'm going to be a teacher, I'm going to be in my own classroom . . . because it's a team thing. . . . We work together." (2005)

Teamwork was an important aspect of the MSMS story from 1998 to 2005, and the team perspective was unique. *Team* at MSMS refers to the individual curriculum and instruction units in the school, to the formal administrative organization, to the faculty efforts to help students, and to the decision-making processes in the school. Even in early interviews, individuals expressed their pleasure at being able to work at MSMS. There seemed to be two reasons for this. Either the teachers liked it at MSMS or they were leary of finding anything similar to it at other campuses. So, one might have seen working at MSMS as good only because other places were not so good.

Regardless of the initial reason, in 2003, the positive feelings of the staff for each other and for the formal leadership in the school seem to have progressed from sporadic to pervasive. In the spring of 2000 one teacher stated:

Well, I think since (Mrs. H's) been here, it's been like that . . . she says if you have a problem, you come to me. Don't let it fester . . . and get larger than it should be. . . . She doesn't want to go through different groups of people for it to finally get to her.

Another example can be seen in this teacher's statement:

I think the morale has gotten better over the years. . . . I think everyone is seen as important; an important part of the puzzle, that everyone contributes regardless of your role or your title. . . . And I think what everyone realizes is that what they do matters and counts. I think that certainly has a positive effect on someone's morale.

In 2003, descriptors that various interviewees used for the culture of the school included the following:

- family.
- dedicated or committed.
- dedicated—everyone involved with student learning.
- don't give up on kids—keep on striving for the best results.
- sincerity.
- generous atmosphere.
- everyone wants to help out, hard working.

There were more such descriptors and many repeated some of those offered here. Although student achievement was almost always voiced as the priority for the school, faculty and staff often added thoughts related to the success of students that went beyond any test or beyond the cognitive dimensions of the MSMS students. It was clear that the MSMS team strived to create students who were successful—not only academically, but beyond academics. Staff mentioned lifelong learning and creating students who were successful in life as important. One teacher said, "teachers touch lives, one day, one lesson at a time." Another commented, "We're interested in our students' learning—students are everything."

To hear such descriptors session after session for two days, no matter with whom you spoke, was a powerful experience. The commitment to children in this school was beyond what we had hoped to find. There was no question that if a strategy did not work for a student, another strategy would be tried. If one person could not get through to a child, other teachers or administrators were sought for assistance. Tests were important, but life success was the real goal. We left wishing that all children could be schooled in such a place, among such professionals.

In our exit from MSMS in December 2003, our impression was that commitment to children and their success was perceived by MSMS staff as a true responsibility. This notion goes beyond merely having a focus on student learning; this is more driven, more inclusive. It seemed to come from the inside-out of the staff. We found references to this phenomenon in interviews with teachers in 2000. The beginnings of this deep individual and school-wide cultural belief about adult relationships and responsibility for student development were heard in comments such as the one made by this teacher when asked about what the staff say is important about their work here:

> Their impact on the students, what they can do in the classroom to reach the students to do their job. We're all willing to cooperate and put in the long hours that it takes.

When asked how people willing to make this commitment were found, another teacher declared:

> Well, when you first start out you either know whether you're going to fit in . . . or you don't. . . . I think it's an automatic thing to know whether you belong somewhere or you don't. If someone sees you're all about work and there's no just laying back.

The teacher went on to say:

> We're very concerned about academics but a lot of times a lot of the teachers here look way beyond that. If the kid's not living up to their academic ability,

we pretty much search beyond that and see maybe what's going on at home or affecting them here at school. We look for other reasons.

Statements from the December 2003 interviews echo the past:

It's a great school to work at. I love coming to school everyday. [We are] very fortunate to have some very qualified teachers that love what they're doing and you can see it. The extra time that teachers and administrators put into what they're doing, I don't think there's a school that works harder than this school. I just feel good about coming and our students, uh, I love our students.

And, from another teacher:

I know that the Mineral Springs Community school district is one of the greatest school districts in the state. . . . It's been a long road getting there, but teachers are wanting to come here because of that reason.

In 2005, a young woman who was promoted from MSMS teacher to MSMS assistant principal gave the following answer when asked, "Are there some teachers that come and this is just not the place for them?"

Oh, maybe one. And it wasn't any[thing] negative. . . . Wished her well, you know. And good recommendations were given. But most people that come here daily, like it here. . . . Most people here are very friendly and [helpful]. They are willing to help you and get you the materials that you need and the mentor teachers are great at doing that.

Also in 2005, the former principal (Mrs. H) and current principal (Mrs. C) commented on MSMS staff's collective responsibility for students. Mrs. H claimed:

You can't just go into your classroom . . . you can't say . . . gee, I'm going to be a teacher, I'm going to be in my own classroom . . . because it's a team thing, . . . we work together . . . whenever we've . . . interviewed people, we say you know we work together . . . is there any reason why you wouldn't be able to work with the teacher next door or across the hall because that's how we work.

The current principal (Mrs. C) reinforced Mrs. H's comments by stating:

Everyday we want everyone to be on duty. . . . When the bell rings, you walk out in the hall, you see a student not doing what he's supposed to be doing . . . you talk to that student. . . . Don't feel like you can't speak to every child that walks up and down the hall. You know, we're in it together and that's what it's all about.

The inclusiveness of the school culture is ubiquitous; this was emphasized in the event described by Mrs. C and affirmed by Mrs. H:

> The custodians here . . . cooked . . . lunch for all the staff . . . to let them know
> they appreciated the teachers. . . . And that's because we include them . . . in
> everything we do, and if we have shirts made . . . they get the shirts. If we
> have gifts to give out, they get gifts and that's even with our cafeteria. We
> actually make them a part of our staff. . . . We just try to make this one big
> happy family.

Similarly, the central office leadership worked to create feelings of inclusiveness as the development of a PLC at the district level was pursued.
One central office administrator identified the following as critically important to this process:

> Involving everybody . . . it wasn't just the department of instruction and
> principals on campuses. It was every department, human resources depart-
> ment . . . made sure that we were recruiting the best teachers that we could
> find. It was the operations department making sure that the schools were in
> good shape. . . . It makes a huge difference. Those people have to be on board
> with it. From the custodians to the cafeteria managers . . . making sure the
> meals they're serving are the best that they can provide. And, athletics, P.E.
> and music and all of that. . . . They tutored kids, just like everybody else did.
> The coaches did, you know everybody was focused around the same pur-
> pose [of] having those kids perform.

Strong collegial relationships and mutual respect in the school were identified by an assistant principal in the 2005 interviews. She was asked if there
was anything unique about this school. She replied, "Just the sense of family. We're like a family, here. Our administrative staff and our teachers are
very understanding . . . it's just a sense of caring throughout the building."
She continued to detail this message when asked what she thought hap-
pens at MSMS to allow students to be so successful year after year:

> I believe it's the teachers and administrators working together. The adminis-
> trators listening to the teachers and the staff . . . listening to their ideas and
> making ways and finding resources necessary. . . . Most teachers are devoted
> to spending long afternoons and showing up on Saturdays to help our stu-
> dents . . . and the students are seeing that the teachers are committed and
> really care about their learning, so that helps build a rapport with the student
> and the teacher.

In our most recent interviews, we found the collaborative culture still
in place. It is clear that working at MSMS has some obvious, but not necessarily spoken expectations, and anyone who is unable to accept and

meet those expectations needs to find another place to work. Anyone who comes to the school and is either unable or unwilling to align themselves with the focus on students' learning and the family culture, soon seeks opportunities elsewhere. As the stories are told, there is no animosity toward those who do not fit, just an acknowledgment that working at MSMS is not for everyone.

Central Office

"The district is a family—a team." (2003)
"Accountability . . . if we're [central office] going to hold them accountable for this, we have to provide the support that they need to do it . . . whatever it takes." (2005)

In the initial interviews in December 1998, the perceived impact of central office was minimal, and focused on decisions regarding staff development. In 2003, however, the principal and assistant principal both commented about their being able to make decisions about staff development at the school level as a new and positive direction for Mineral Springs.

In 2003, central office was viewed positively. It was seen as a support rather than a barrier to the work of the school. From field notes of these interviews, many people spoke positively of the central office at all levels. An assistant principal said, "Central office is very supportive. This is what sets us apart from other districts. Our administration gets us what we need. This is the message passed down from our superintendent."

Instructional specialists were most often mentioned when asked about the support from central office for the campus. Some of these instructional specialists were previously MSMS teachers. Also mentioned was that many individuals from this school have moved to central office positions or positions of leadership in other schools. This history appears to have contributed to the strong central office-to-campus links and the positive PK–12 campus interactions. References to these strong positive relationships were heard again in the 2005 interviews. A social studies department chair was asked if she thought the instructional specialists from central office had an impact on student achievement at the school:

I do. . . . They know what we're supposed to be covering to make the student successful and they visit the classrooms on a regular basis and if they see that anyone is having a problem . . . it's a matter of coming to the department chair and saying, you know . . . so and so seems to be having a problem. They then could work within that area . . . so it's more helpful.

In recounting the improvement process in the district, one of the central office administrators who was instrumental in this effort spoke about some of the major steps taken in getting things moving across the district:

We trimmed our budgets at central office by 30 percent and put that money
out on campuses. We provided instructional specialists for each campus, we
provided the technology instructional specialists who help them. . . . We developed . . . district assessments . . . an assessment to inform instruction . . .
so you know where kids are, at any given time.

He described the overall philosophy that was used in developing the
central office-campus relationship in this long-term district-wide improvement process:

You build accountability and then you provide support for the accountability. . . . If we're going to hold them accountable for this we have to provide
the support that they need to do it . . . whatever it takes.

MEETING THE CHALLENGE

The four themes of focus, leadership, relationships, and central office
emerged in the earliest data from our work at this school and continued
to be present as evidenced in the interviews in 2005. Over this decade of
study, it is apparent that while the themes remained constant none of
them developed smoothly; each seems to have had times of little or no
progress and some even have had periods of regression.

Focus appears to have been the most consistent of the themes. From
1998 through 2005, teachers and administrators voiced the consistent
message that MSMS was about student learning. In 1998, the measure of
that learning was narrowly defined as scores on the state-mandated tests;
in 2005, state tests were still used as measures but began also to include
indicators such as activities involvement, behavior issues, school and career ambitions, and enjoyment of learning.

The early probes in 1998 generated the somewhat surprising theme
regarding how central office was perceived at MSMS (i.e., "central office
is generally viewed as a positive assist to the school's instructional efforts").

Since that time, the researchers' curiosity, other research in which they
have engaged, and the growing literature regarding the importance of
district support for change to occur, encouraged a return to MSMS in May
of 2005 to interview central office personnel. Generally the positive perspective of central office is still heard; however, there are clues that this
may be changing. Already mentioned was the assistant principal's response that changes in the superintendency and central office were disruptive to "everything." Another hint comes in this quote: "[I]n the past
. . . every school could do what they needed to do to get going and now a
lot of it is, you know, top down."

The changes in the district's rating based on the state testing also creates curiosity about why this may have occurred; could it be related to leadership succession, instructional strategies and program changes brought in with the new administration, less emphasis on student learning as measured by state tests, or possibly a reduction in support from central office? Certainly these are questions worth pondering and perhaps investigating.

Another of the early themes concentrated on the relationships between and among the various personnel at MSMS. From the earliest to the most recent interviews, it was absolutely clear that people who worked at MSMS were happy to be at the school. These positive relationships continue as prominent influences in the school. It was learned during the early visits that many individuals in the school had feelings about their work at MSMS that went far beyond job satisfaction to a level of joy. In some instances, teachers in the school were former students of the school; they specifically mentioned individuals still in the school who inspired them to become teachers.

In the 2005 interviews these strong positive feelings about working at MSMS continued to be expressed. All of those interviewed during the 2005 visit echoed sentiments about the school's powerful family culture. There really was general optimism toward the continued improvement of the school's performance with the appointment of a new school leader. On the other hand, how the development at the district level might unfold seemed to be viewed less optimistically.

Lastly, it is obvious that the theme of leadership has been a powerful influence on MSMS and the district as a whole. The quality and strength of leadership at both the campus and district levels have alternated between times of stability and times of change.

Our 2005 return to Mineral Springs was important in learning more about the impact of the major changes at the central office. The leadership succession issues at central office were beginning to generate some dissonance within the school and the district. Although strong central office leadership and support were viewed early on as crucial in the school's and district's improvement processes, more recent comments focused on a greater degree of centralizing of decision making and leadership changes that were viewed as disruptive rather than supportive. Even though the new superintendent had been in the office for only a year when we last visited, influences on the school's operations were already being assessed. Also, though the new principal for MSMS had not been selected during our 2005 visit, the positive improvements reported in the student testing data found in Table 9.2 may indicate that a positive succession move was made in the hiring of this individual.

Leadership, or a lack of it, has always been and will always be a factor in individual and organizational development. MSMS is no exception.

ANALYZING PROFESSIONAL
LEARNING COMMUNITY PRACTICES

1. Locate evidence from the story that is related to the following PLC dimensions:

   - Shared and supportive leadership

     ▪ What events, both inside and outside the school, helped build leadership capacity at Mineral Springs?

   - Shared values and vision

     ▪ Does Mineral Springs have a vision? What is it? How was it created? Has it changed at all from 1998 to 2005? Why do you say that?

   - Collective learning and application

     ▪ Do teachers at Mineral Springs engage in collective learning and application of that learning? Has the content or sources of collective learning changed from 1998 to 2005?

   - Supportive conditions—structures

     ▪ What structures were created that supported Mineral Springs development as a PLC?

   - Supportive conditions—relationships

     ▪ Describe the continuum of relationships from classroom teacher to superintendent as supportive conditions in Mineral Springs and the district.

2. Identify examples from the story that:

   - Explain how focusing on high expectations for student success has been reflected in teacher actions.
   - Give details that explain teacher feelings of satisfaction.
   - Illustrate how leadership succession impacted PLC development in the school.
   - Describe the role central office played in the development of Mineral Springs as a PLC.

3. Relate this case story to your own school, regarding the following areas:

   - Leadership succession: Is leadership succession important at your school? Why?
     Vision development: How was the vision developed in your school? What words would best describe your school's focus?
     Collective learning: Does collective learning occur in your school? If so, how does it align with your school's mission and improvement plans?
     Involved central office: Does central office impact student learning in your school? Why do you say that?
     Strong relationships: Offering suggestions on how you would create and maintain these positive feelings in your school.

4. How would you use the following tools to establish or redirect reforms at your school?

   - The PLCO
   - The PLC-ICM
   - The ESS-ICM
   - The PLCDR
   - The Initial PLC Plan

10

✦

Case Study #3

Ralph H. Metcalfe School (K4–8)

Linda C. Roundtree and Kristine Kiefer Hipp

INTRODUCTION

Ralph H. Metcalfe School is a year-round public school located in the central city of Milwaukee. As a neighborhood school, it serves approximately 355 students in K4–Grade 8 and their families in the Todd Wehr Metcalfe Park community.

Metcalfe opened as a new school in the fall of 2000. In an effort to provide programming that would best address students' cognitive and affective needs, the school shares space with the Roger and Leona Fitzsimonds Boys and Girls Club. This dual use of the site and community partnership supports comprehensive programming to address the needs of the whole child. This was the first public school nationally to have a Boys and Girls Club as a part of its facility.

Metcalfe is one of 212 schools within the Milwaukee Public Schools (MPS). Of the 88,000 students enrolled in MPS during the 2007–2008 school year, 88 percent were students of color, 78 percent were eligible for free and reduced lunch, 18 percent were students with special needs, and student mobility was approximately 20 percent. From year to year, the student mobility rate averages about 35 percent district wide. In comparison to the district-wide data, Metcalfe's student enrollment demographic data are more profound than that for the district. Over 98 percent of its students in 2007–2008 were African American, over 95 percent were eligible for free and reduced lunch, and 23 percent were identified as having special needs.

Tables 10.1 and 10.2 illustrate staff and student demographics respectively. Unlike most MPS schools, the staff is reflective of the students in

demographic makeup. Approximately 80 percent of the teachers and support staff are African American.

Table 10.1   Ralph H. Metcalfe Elementary School: Staff Demographics*

	Male	Fem	American Indian	African American	Asian	Hispanic	White	Other
Teachers PreK–8	4	13	0	14	0	0	3	0
Paraprofessionals	1	5	0	5	0	0	1	0
Teachers Special Ed	0	5	0	4	0	0	1	0

* Data obtained from the Wisconsin Department of Public Instruction website: http://dpi.state.wi.us/sig/index
.html.

Table 10.2   Ralph H. Metcalfe Elementary School: Student Demographics*

	R.H. Metcalfe	School District
All Pupils	306	
Yearly Attendance (%)	87.9	
Gender		
Female (%)	50.0	
Male (%)	50.0	
Race		
American Indian (%)	0.0	
Asian (%)	0.3	
African American (%)	97.4	
Hispanic (%)	0.3	
White (%)	2.0	
Subsidized Lunch		
Eligible (%)	92.2	
Special Needs:		
With Disabilities (%)	18.6	
Languages		
Spanish	N/A	
Hmong	N/A	
Other	N/A	
English (%)	100	

*Data includes yearly attendance, special needs: 2005–2006 and gender, ethnicity, subsidized lunch,
languages: 2006–2007.
Note: Data obtained from the Wisconsin Department of Public Instruction website: http://dpi.state.wi.us/sig/
index.html.

PRINCIPAL'S INITIAL REFLECTIONS

Unlike the previous two case stories, we capitalize on insights from our principal-author who contributes firsthand information regarding her initial reflections in assuming the role of principal at Metcalfe. Such reflections are rarely captured and we feel it is important during times of leadership succession.

Upon my arrival as principal at Ralph H. Metcalfe in 2006, there were several obstacles that confronted me related to student achievement, staff morale, professional development, and the culture of the school. The school was at risk, chaotic, unsafe, and not conducive to student learning. Staff morale was extremely low. Several teachers threatened to leave or requested a transfer. Student enrollment had declined from 450 to approximately 295 students. The attendance of staff was worse than that of the students, and it was apparent that many were ready to leave, not only the school, but also the profession. They had given up hope. The culture and climate were disheartening.

Also, all of the specialty teachers had transferred to other schools. Despite being a new building that included a partnership with the Boys and Girls Club, the school was barely meeting the academic, social, or emotional needs of the children. Reflecting on this culture, two important questions emerged. First, what would a principal need to do right away to create a positive school culture? Second, what was the best way to build staff and student morale in a timely manner? Of course all of this would aid me in building capacity within the staff as well.

Instead of focusing on the enormity of the challenges, the MPS report card data was reviewed as a way to gain background information and identify critical areas of need. The data included mobility rates, truancy data, suspension rates, and assessment results. These data became critical to envision a brighter future for Metcalfe's students and staff.

As principal, I was especially interested in *beacons of hope*, or areas in which the school was doing really well, despite the challenges it faced. It was imperative that teachers and the entire school community needed to be positively stroked if meaningful changes were to occur.

An initial plan was immediately developed as to how the school community would be addressed individually and collectively. Next, scheduled meetings were arranged with the learning team (steering committee), school governance council, and the parent-teacher organization

(PTO). Additionally, a get-acquainted question-and-answer session was conducted for those new to the school community.

These initial meetings were received very well. All stakeholders, including teachers, paraprofessionals, parents/guardians, and community partners, heard my vision for the school and asked questions relative to implementing recommended strategies and practices. The staff supported the vision because they too saw the larger picture: high academic success for all could truly be attained. As we embraced a shared vision we were able to enjoy a very productive and successful first year.

Year 1

Creating a PLC, capitalizing upon the strengths of every team member, and high academic achievement were at the top of the list. Holding staff accountable, building capacity within staff, and advocating for children were crucial elements to help close the achievement gaps. Knowing the morale of students and staff were relatively low, goal setting, data reflection, and self-evaluation were some of the first stepping stones used to build a sense of community. These tools provided the basis to which we established an effective learning team to benchmark our growth on a bi-weekly basis.

Our goals included establishing a vision and mission statement we as a staff would know, communicate, and value. The ultimate goal was to create and sustain positive momentum, secure high staff morale, model strategies to demonstrate the importance of advocating for children, and focus professional development to meet the diverse needs of both students and staff.

Finally, we targeted parental involvement. We wanted parents to be aware of the curriculum, support their child at home by reinforcing appropriate strategies, and share responsibility in holding their children accountable for high academic success.

Year 2

During our second year (2007–2008), Metcalfe staff collectively established a mission that served as the foundation for our efforts:

> The Metcalfe staff is committed to making informed curriculum decisions based on data. We use high-yield, research-based instructional strategies to differentiate instruction to meet the diverse learning styles of Metcalfe students. Dedicated to providing real world challenges and experiences, we infuse current technology into instructional practices throughout the school community. We accomplish this within a safe environment conducive to learning in collaboration with families and community partners, such as

SPARK (a literacy program), our Community Learning Center (CLC) and the Fitzsimonds Boys and Girls Club. By implementing the mission, Metcalfe staff is committed to providing all students with educational opportunities that will promote and sustain their ability to be proficient or advanced on all Wisconsin Academic and Social-Emotional Standards, prepare them for the rigors and challenges of high school, and lead them to a variety of post-secondary educational or career opportunities.

The staff were committed to the mission and shared vision of the school and a stronger sense of community was evident. Data became the primary vehicle from which we gained a sense of hope (see Figure 10.1).

By consistently examining and reflecting on our data we were able to group our students based on their needs, provide additional support to those who scored below proficiency, and strive to become an instructional culture. Students were grouped in tiers. These tiers provided the structure to remediate students who were in most need and challenge those who scored at or above proficiency on standardized tests. In addition, we found our regular celebrations of students and staff were invaluable. Staff meetings (professional development days) were instrumental in provid-

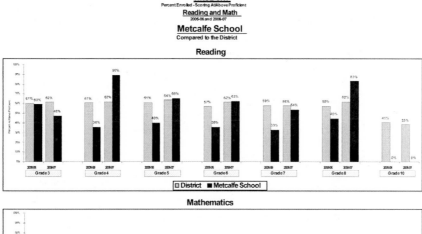

Figure 10.1.

ing staff with time to network and collaborate around curricular issues. Scheduling collaborative time for teachers was essential.

Although Metcalfe has K4 students, the Student Achievement Guarantee in Education (SAGE) program begins at K5, in which classrooms are funded through a state initiative to address student achievement in the early grades. Such classrooms have a maximum 15-to-1 student-teacher ratio.

As a result of the high percentage of students receiving free or reduced lunch, the school also receives federal Title I funds to further support and promote student achievement and parental involvement. SAGE and Title I funds also help to provide additional human and material resources to enrich and enhance the school's curriculum and promote parental and community involvement. These funds all support the No Child Left Behind (NCLB) mandate that all educators provide high-quality instruction to significantly increases student achievement.

THE STORY

Most school reform research states that true reform usually takes 3 to 5 years to take root and grow. In many ways, Ralph H. Metcalfe School is an exception to this general body of research. It has undergone successful and significant reform within the past 2 years as a result of strong and passionate principal leadership, a dedicated staff with high expectations engaged in meaningful professional development, a positive climate and culture focused on student achievement, and external support systems. The following story reveals key themes that have impacted the culture of the school over the past two years and the journey it took to create change.

Strong and Passionate Principal Leadership

It took almost a full year for the staff to trust my leadership. They now describe it as *passionate* and *dedicated*—two elements deemed necessary in creating a PLC. Over that first year, the staff opened to new ideas and strategies that empower everyone to be advocates for children.

As an instructional leader, I worked closely with the learning team, a group of individuals representing each grade level and department whose primary purpose is working toward improving teaching and learning. We met frequently to analyze school data and provide direction for the writing and implementation of our educational plan designed to improve instruction.

As principal, I spent countless hours in the classrooms demonstrating instructional practices and also conducting workshops with the staff on key curricular issues. Teachers welcomed the opportunity to see best practices modeled and to access additional professional development opportunities on effective research-based strategies. Several avenues were created for staff to network, examine data, and discuss potential strategies to meet the students' most urgent needs. Professional development was embedded in the school day to allow for flexibility and participation. It was tailored to the needs of the staff by grade level and was always followed with reflection and dialogue.

In time, teachers began modeling research-based strategies for peers. They improved staff morale as they encouraged each other through this type of interaction. Buy-in was at an all-time high when peers led specific meetings and staff were given opportunities to collaborate and reflect on their teaching experiences. Collaborative structures were numerous; therefore all teachers had to demonstrate leadership by co-chairing committees, scheduling literacy-based parent events, and creating ways to celebrate student success. Staff received the personal recognition they deserved and often commented as to how positive and uplifting this made them feel.

Staff were also encouraged to engage in local and district professional development to increase their present skill level performance. When they returned from these sessions, opportunities were made available for staff to share with their colleagues and engage in focused conversations. What a valuable learning experience there was as staff continued to attend meaningful sessions!

As a staff we set goals as to what we hoped to attain by the end of each year. Evaluation of our progress toward those goals was ongoing. We consistently monitored the impact it had on student achievement.

"Let's Chat" sessions replaced the old monitoring conferences to create a safe environment and exchange practices. These sessions initially were held individually and later jointly by grade levels. Teachers developed trust as they shared student data and work, thus becoming more transparent about their professional needs. The information shared during the Let's Chat sessions drove the agenda for staff development and developed more sustained and cohesive units by grade level.

Things were finally moving in a positive direction as teachers exhibited a sense of responsibility and accountability. Passionate and dedicated leadership was *also* highly evident in staff as they competently initiated practices related to student learning.

Dedicated Staff, High Expectations, and Professional Development

Apparently, Metcalfe has always had a dedicated staff committed to academic achievement and the well-being of children, but prior to 2006, conversations centered on low student achievement, safety issues, discipline, and low parental involvement. Progress was minimal and the staff was exhausted and devastated by the lack of support. The staff needed a great deal of assistance in reaching their goals for the children. This became my first priority after arriving as principal.

As the staff became confident that they would receive the support needed, there was a noticeable change in staff and student morale. In fact, the climate changed altogether. Within a month after working collaboratively with staff, parents, and the Boys and Girls Club, this staff expressed that they *regained hope*.

In a few short months, the staff's purpose, dedication, and commitment increased in focus and depth. Academic progress was the number one priority for all students. The teachers received professional development from the curriculum generalist and the principal before taking on a similar responsibility. Instruction using Bloom's Taxonomy was a common thread across each classroom. This was critical to the success we celebrated in our first year because all teachers consistently held students accountable for learning. Teaching higher level thinking skills and challenging students to actively participate in their learning, analyze their own work, and apply what they learned quickly became the norm.

Through the daily commitment of the entire staff, students were inspired to work strategically to reach their individual goals. Teacher involvement in learning took front stage as they became actively engaged in facilitating discussions and demonstrating strategies they used to solve problems. Students also took ownership within their classroom in varied leadership roles during the reading and language arts block.

Conversations within the classroom changed so much that positive comments from parents and other stakeholders quickly traveled within the district. Staff openly commented, "This was why I came into teaching," "I finally got my groove back," and "I didn't know if I would ever feel the same again."

Teacher expectations for urban students were realistic and high enough to allow them to achieve at equal or higher levels than those of their suburban and rural peers. With this mindset, we placed a strong focus on facilitating staff conversations around the academic expectations for *all* students. To increase the number of students meeting or exceeding proficiency, these conversations were connected to the state standards, the district's learning targets and characteristics of high-performing urban classrooms, and research-based strategies that prove to address various student learning modalities and produce high academic results to close achievement gap.

As a result of the unwavering efforts of teachers, students have risen to the occasion as they are provided clear expectations, coupled with academic support during and after school. Students are now on a path to high academic progress as they strive to work to their fullest potential.

To increase student morale and promote active engagement, the staff showcases student work samples along with the related learning target(s). Metcalfe is transforming into an oasis of learning! Visitors walk through and make comments about how professional the students' work looks and about the positive changes due to our commitment. Also, teachers receive written praise in weekly staff bulletins, and teacher of the month recognition, certificates, and audio announcements celebrating staff *and* students.

Measuring the benefits of such a school-wide effort is a process within itself. Learning walks, or walkthroughs, are used as an observation and feedback tool. During a learning walk, the administrator is able to see if students are engaged in the learning process and to gauge whether the conversations in the classroom are student-centered, teacher-led, or student-led. Additionally, it is helpful to take note of the instructional strategies and types of assessment used during instruction, and the levels of Bloom's Taxonomy addressed—a predominant focus for student instruction and engagement.

Within a brief time, a snapshot of the teacher's instructional strategies is visible and modifications are made to meet the diverse learning needs of students. It is then that we are able to provide hands-on learning experiences, and engage students in the learning process at higher levels (i.e., analysis, synthesis, and evaluation). Students are empowered to be in control of the learning process and respond in ways that defend or support their thought processes in an effective manner.

Our Let's Chat sessions also drive professional development, now embedded into grade-level-specific and peer-led experiences. Professional development is ongoing, differentiated, highly effective, and embraced as the staff is adding to the repertoire of skills they can readily implement into their classrooms.

The learning team took responsibility for planning the professional development and created rubrics to ensure the effectiveness of professional development received. Professional development is also evaluated for its impact on student achievement and teachers' instructional practices. What a tremendous difference this has made at Metcalfe!

Staff meetings are now gateways to new ways of focusing on collective learning where sharing best practices takes center court. Grade-level unit teachers present while the rest of the staff play the role of students. The looks on their faces when they present are unforgettable. Nervousness has been dispelled and confidence is projected.

Professional development is ongoing, authentic, and data-driven. We call this strategy an *assessment for learning* because our paradigms have shifted from assessment *of* learning to assessment *for* learning.

To build a sense of collegiality across grade levels, a schedule was created for teachers to meet weekly and collaborate around curricular issues and data. During this time, each individual has something to contribute no matter how great or small. Sharing the same common language and goals are obviously stepping stones to cohesiveness. The staff reflect what a true learning environment should look, feel, and sound like. When asked to implement strategies, take on a new role, or facilitate a parent forum, teams collaborate, share ideas, get feedback, and flow with a spirit of excellence.

As the children are our priority, time and time again staff spend hours reflecting and seeking out best practices. Most powerfully, the lives of our children are being transformed academically, socially, and emotionally as a result of teachers changing their instructional and communication practices to better meet students' diverse cognitive and affective needs.

A Positive Climate and Culture Focused on Student Achievement

As an administrator, I strongly believe that the culture in one's building is very much dependent on the attitude and leadership of the principal. Therefore, the tone in our building is set for academic success to occur on a daily basis by creating an environment that supports a belief in the potential of all students. Yes, we must believe all students can, will, and must learn. Pride is reflected by setting the stage for success to happen daily.

To facilitate this, I initially build and foster hope within my staff and, in return, ask that they do the same for each of the students' lives that they will touch. Creating a sense of hope in the adults motivates them to develop and maintain confidence and high expectations for increasing student achievement. It also instills within them the need to be lifelong learners. It is for this reason the staff's needs are seriously considered as they relate to curriculum and instruction. And, based on our needs assessments, we seek to build capacity within all individuals at Metcalfe. Also, by *sharing the reality*—the achievement data—with staff, it is possible to more effectively communicate the vision and create an awareness of the process it will take to reach the vision of a strong instructional culture together.

The old adage is true: "Together we can make a difference." Therefore, it is critical for staff to realize they are the beacons of hope for all students. To promote this belief, individual staff members are recognized on a monthly basis for outstanding and commendable effort. As principal, I frequently observe the positive impact such recognition has on staff members and how those not recognized are motivated to strive harder on behalf of their students. What an inspiration! Just imagine the impact this has on student learning.

Students excel in different ways. The more resources a school has that focus on supporting student achievement, the greater potential there is for an increase in students' success.

Considering the repressive conditions that some students encounter before coming to us each day, they need praise and affirmation on a daily basis. It must be consistent and ongoing because it impacts the learning environment and achievement of all students. Not only does the staff play a role in delivering praise and affirmation to the students, but I also make it my business to encourage students to do their best both in and outside of the classroom. I begin and end each day by meeting with the school community as a whole giving students direct words of encouragement and also place a priority on visiting with them at lunch.

Students are taught to set goals, take pride in daily attendance, respect and appreciate cultural differences, and take control of their learning through effective organization and a strong commitment to academic excellence. Parents are invited to join as partners to enforce these same guidelines and assist their children at home with the numerous tips we provide in communiqués.

I value my time with the students because it helps the teachers and students to acknowledge my worth as a caring, concerned, and engaged team player. It is my hope, as an administrator, to help to improve and change my students' lives and outlooks one day at a time while setting before them positive examples, excellent role models, tangible incentives, and beacons of hope.

External Support Systems

Dedicated to providing real-world challenges and experiences, we also infuse current technology into instructional practices throughout the school community through partnership with Spheres of Proud Achievement in Reading for Kids (SPARK, a literacy program in collaboration with UW-Milwaukee to close achievement gaps), the CLC, and the Fitzsimonds Boys and Girls Club.

These collaborative efforts offer a variety of programs specifically for intervention with students who are below level in reading and language arts. SPARK, CLC, and the Boys and Girls Club offer tutorial during and after school. SPARK focuses on the students in grades K5–3 reading below grade level as measured on the classroom assessments based on standards, anticipating how they would perform on the WKCE at grades 3–8. The other partners target their tutorial support to all grades and all subjects.

Our partners are helping us to build the bridge to create systemic and lasting change, remembering always that the bottom line, the urgency, is student learning.

With these external supports, differentiated instruction and flexible grouping have proven to be highly successful. At Metcalfe, the five components of reading instruction in a balanced literacy approach were embedded through our 2-hour language arts block. In all content areas, reading strategies were practiced, student learning styles addressed, and activities varied to meet students' needs. This is our greatest resource in helping us move instruction from the theoretical base to practical application.

Moreover, we formed healthy partnerships with the Boys and Girls Club to address the students' academic needs through tutorials. The Boys and Girls Club also provided a safe haven for them to engage in extracurricular activities in a nurturing environment.

Alverno College was also a collaborative force in providing professional development for our staff surrounding the needs of our children. Staff met monthly at the college in focused areas, concentrating their energies on improving the academic performance of all students. Also, monthly sessions are held with parents at all grade levels to familiarize them with best practices used within the classroom.

Other meaningful relationships with community partners include Second Harvest, which provided supplies for the students. In addition LensCrafters gave vision exams and glasses to children free of charge. Columbia St. Mary's Hospital donated time and attention to the dental care of our children. Lisbon Association Neighborhood Development (LAND) was a vital partner in making it possible for children to visit, firsthand, several key sites in Wisconsin, participate in a service learning project, and create multimedia presentations to share their experiences. These are all valued partners who add to the academic success our children now enjoy.

MEETING THE CHALLENGE

As a school such as Metcalfe moves closer to a Blue Ribbon status, there are critical challenges we must face. One challenge includes principal succession and its impact on the sustainability of teacher efforts and efficacy. Another challenge is the continuous achievement gap in mathematics. Finally, we must expand our external support to meet the vision of academic proficiency in every child.

I worked with this awesome staff for 2 consecutive years and was asked to take over as principal of Roosevelt Middle School of the Arts. It was no secret change would occur; however, the most important element was sustainability. The staff had worked smarter to become a model PLC, one in which they valued and were proud to be active members. Knowing the staff and their contributions, hope was renewed and conversation began with the new administrator.

Realizing that academic growth was a top priority, discussions were aimed at mathematics where there was minimal or no growth made. Prior to leaving, the staff and I came up with a plan to restructure classrooms to allow for more flexibility. All teachers would work on this content area and capitalize upon each teachable moment. Math problems of the week were developed, increased opportunities to utilize constructive responses were created, and clear communication existed between our staff and our external partners around mathematics.

Can this discussion continue at the level initiated? Not only was this a possible challenge; rather it led to another concern, expanding external support to meet the vision of academic proficiency in every child. Would the new principal arrive with an agenda of her own? Would Metcalfe continue to thrive as it had begun these last few years or at its initial opening? The most important question lingers, how will Metcalfe meet the challenge?

While I am leaving to assume responsibilities at another school, I am comforted knowing the potential exists. Leadership capacity and continuous learning have developed to not only sustain the gains made but to also lead students to new heights.

ANALYZING PROFESSIONAL
LEARNING COMMUNITY PRACTICES:

1. Generate evidence related to the following PLC dimensions:

- Shared and supportive leadership

  - How was leadership capacity created, shared, and implemented?

- Shared values and vision

  - How were school efforts aligned to the school's vision, values, and goals?

- Collective learning and application

  - How were the staff involved in focused and meaningful learning?

- Shared personal practice

- How did teachers share their practice?

- Supportive conditions—relationships

  - How were relationships of trust and respect established?

- Supportive conditions—structures

  - How were structures established that support the culture of the PLC?

- External factors

  - To what degree was the entire school community engaged?

2. Identify examples from the story that:

   - Cite examples of *strong* and *passionate* principal leadership that:
     - Demonstrates how the principal built leadership capacity.
     - Reflect how a positive climate and culture promoted high-quality teaching and learning.
     - Reveal evidence of how staff demonstrated: (a) collaboration, (b) leadership, and (c) a commitment to high expectations to improve student learning?
     - Indicate how meaningful external support systems (parents and community members) interacted with the school as a PLC?
     - Demonstrate intentional planning for sustainability.

3. Relate this case story to your own school, regarding the following areas:

   - Strong and passionate leadership: Share evidence that supports strong and passionate leadership in your school if it exists. Is the vision aligned with the outcomes of your school's mission?
   - Dedicated staff with high expectations: How was the vision developed in your school? What words would best describe your school's focus?
   - Positive climate and culture: How does collective learning occur in your school to create an instructional culture? If so, how does learning align with your school's mission and improvement plans?
   - External support systems: How do the interactions among central office personnel, parents, and community members impact student learning in your school? What evidence can you provide?

- Strong relationships: What strategies are working in your school to develop strong relationships across stakeholders? How is respect and trust fostered and nurtured in your school?
- Leadership succession: How is leadership succession approached at your school? Share specific examples as to how leaders are being prepared to assume greater leadership responsibility.

4. How would you use the following tools to establish or redirect reforms at your school?

- The PLCO
- The PLC-ICM
- The ESS-ICM
- The PLCDR
- The Initial PLC Plan

11

Sustainability

A Constant Process for Continuing Improvement

Anita M. Pankake, Jesus Abrego, and Gayle Moller

Imagine Yourself...

You are at the airport or perhaps one of those really fancy hotels we like to dream about staying for a relaxing weekend. You have your bags trailing behind you—on rollers, of course. You may also have one or two "personal items" hanging from your shoulders. You are ready—you have arrived—you are on your way! As you approach the entrance, you see one of those revolving doors that some thoughtful engineer has designed so that you (and your bags) step in with plenty of space to accommodate. If you start moving forward, close to but not touching the glass panel in front of you, it moves forward, just a bit ahead of you. If you move too fast, get too close, or stop walking, the door stops moving and you are caught inside. As you look around to make sure all of your "stuff" is in line, step back, pause, and then move forward again—slowly, at a measured pace—the door again begins to move. You are back on track, engaging in ways that permit the door to draw you forward and move you toward your targeted destination!

The image of a revolving door can elicit various connotations. It may imply that people are coming and going, but not staying, or that no progress is being made, you are just moving in circles. For us, however, we want you as a reader to view this image metaphorically to consider the necessary conditions for sustaining a PLC. In this chapter, we use the power of metaphor to simulate decisions and actions that promote sustainability.

According to Datnow (2005), "when one speaks of the sustainability of a reform, one is typically interested in knowing whether the reform lasts over time and becomes an institutionalized feature of a school. For a reform to be sustained, it must become institutionalized. So, too, when a reform is institutionalized, it has been sustained over time" (p. 123). Furthermore, Crowther and colleagues (cited in Andrews and Lewis, 2004) added that "sustaining is about building on the knowledge that has been created now into the future. It is about continual refinement and the building of enhanced identity and capacity" (p. 137).

The previous chapters have given you the concepts and tools needed to take purposeful actions to generate the positive results that come with the initiation and implementation of a PLC in your school. If you apply what has been suggested in these chapters, you increase the probability that you will facilitate change.

A major issue in the literature on change in organizations deals with how to sustain the changes once they are implemented, which is the focus of this chapter. The case story of Mineral Springs illustrates this challenge when years of succession planning end and several leaders leave the school and district. How can you be assured that the positive results you have accrued are maintained? What continuing actions do you need to take to, not only maintain, but also continue to improve and innovate? What are some of the challenges that must be addressed if your good work is not to be undone? And what are some of the new resources and supports that may be needed as your school continues to mature as a PLC?

To address these questions we have developed seven actions that, if taken, will increase the likelihood that the positive results you have achieved will be sustained and even improved.

These actions are based on the dimensions of a PLC, the heart of this book. There is a recommended action for each of these dimensions (shared values and vision, shared and supportive leadership, collective learning and application, shared personal practice, and supportive conditions, which features two parts—structures and relationships and external support systems). For each we first offer a concise statement of action followed by a brief discussion applying the concepts and tools presented in previous chapters. We conclude each section with some suggestions or examples of ways to implement the recommended actions.

We also want you to continue to think of that revolving door image as an organizer for what you are doing and why you are doing it to meet the continuing challenges required of sustainability.

SHARED VALUES AND VISION

Make sure that the vision is always on the horizon.

In our image of the revolving door, if you touch it, the door stops and you are caught inside—not making progress. You have to move forward, but you must also let the door lead you. So it is also with sustaining a PLC. Although the vision and values must be shared by those involved in implementing them, the vision, particularly, must always be a bit ahead of where you are. If you assume that you can reach your vision you will, as a school, be stopped and caught inside without being able to move forward. To prevent this, the school's vision, mission, and values must be revisited periodically.

A vision is always where you want to be. Remember, you can achieve your goals and objectives, but not your vision. It is your vision that you must continually walk toward but never quite reach.

If your school is good, it can be better; and, if you work collectively toward your vision, your school can be great! There is no *end* to learning for either the students or adults in a learning community. Make sure that everyone—students, staff, and parents—understands that we never *arrive*, we only continue the journey.

A list of things you might do to create shared values and vision follows:

- Establish shared values that pull people together at the heart level and remind them why they are here. Post the values on every door of every room and office and maintain accountability.
- Confirm that high expectations for student achievement are a priority for teaching and learning.
- Hold whole school and grade-level group meetings at the beginning, middle, and end of each year to affirm or revise the vision for the school.
- Post the shared vision and mission in a variety of locations throughout the school.
- Model and ask the following question in response to any idea or proposed change for the school: "How does that help us move toward the vision of our school?"
- Return to the vision, which is where you find common ground and find what you care about most, especially when faced with personnel conflicts and diverse opinions emerge.
- Schedule a retreat periodically (probably every 3 to 5 years, but more often if your situation requires it) to revise or reaffirm the school's vision, mission, and shared values.

SHARED AND SUPPORTIVE LEADERSHIP

Embed leadership as a quality in the organization, not just in individuals.

In our image of the revolving door, you are walking forward at a slow, measured pace. This action ensures that you are doing what is necessary to make steady progress toward your destination. If you have ever actually been in one of these doors, you know that even when you are taking appropriate action, it is difficult to do it alone. What about the person behind you or the one in front of you? If they do not take the necessary action as well, it does not really matter that you are, the door will stop and you will all be caught inside.

In the school, this means that everyone has to know what needs to be done, know how it needs to be done, and also, be willing to take the initiative to do it. It means that leadership is everywhere and expected of everyone—in classrooms, in policy development, in program adoption and evaluation, in the larger community, and in personal development; it is a dynamic of the school, not a position in the school. Leadership is supportive; it is reciprocal in offering to others and expecting from others the responsibility and accountability of doing what is right.

In the revolving door, you cannot complete the actions for others. That is also true in the school. You must confidently share the responsibility for doing the right things and hold high standards for accountability for everyone in the school—adults and students. Getting through the door successfully and sustaining the positive results of a professional community require that everyone does his or her part, sometimes this means leading, other times following. However, it is most important that everyone is in the right place and doing the right things to ensure everyone's progress.

The following actions are helpful in incorporating shared leadership in your school:

- Provide induction for new faculty that helps them learn the culture and decision-making processes of the school.
- Use every opportunity to share authority and responsibility with staff.
- Emphasize that all staff are accountable for student learning.
- Use facilitation skills more often that directive behavior in working with staff. Teach them. Do not assume that those who take on leadership responsibilities can skillfully facilitate change.
- Develop a purposeful succession plan by nurturing leaders who influence attitudes and practices aligned to the school's improvement plan.
- Engage central office personnel in supporting your succession plan.

COLLECTIVE LEARNING AND APPLICATION

Learn and work together in new ways.

Do you recall the first time you walked through a revolving door? Perhaps you were the one who put your hand on the door or walked too fast and caused things to stall. No doubt someone either in front of or behind you gave you feedback on what to do in order for things to work. The next time you faced the challenge of such an endeavor you knew what to do and perhaps gave someone else the feedback that they needed to improve their skill in maneuvering this challenge.

So it is with sustaining the PLC work accomplished in the school. Some teachers know what to do, whereas others do not. Those who know share information with others so that little by little everyone's knowledge and skills improve. Knowledge and skills increase more rapidly when you get feedback and correctives on your performance and learn new strategies from someone who already knows how things work. Teaching can be an isolated endeavor in which we can get stuck if we do not have others to assist us. Sometimes by trial and error we can manage to figure out a way to make things work, but it is much more efficient and less frightening if someone helps us.

When teachers and administrators in the school learn and work together on ways to improve instruction and the school environment, more students learn more. It is important that collective learning and application continue if the PLC is to be sustained. Even individual teachers who have exceptional skills can learn new strategies, become more knowledgeable in content, and find new ways of interacting with colleagues that assist their individual work and improve conditions for others. Even schools that are doing well look for ways to improve student performance; being successful does not prevent these schools from becoming more successful (DuFour, DuFour, Eaker, & Karhanek, 2004; Reeves, 2006). It is a reflection of this perspective that needs to be the mantra of a school committed to continually improving conditions for teaching and learning.

To sustain collective learning and related application, you may consider learning and working together in new ways to meet the following goals:

- Initiate study groups with staff. These can focus on books, research, or assessing student work.
- Work with staff in assessing student learning needs and then selecting and planning professional development activities to address those needs.
- Provide conditions to allow implementation of newly learned skills by providing the following three phases to all professional development:

    - Phase 1: Preplan with staff regarding why professional development is important to the work of the school and set objectives for what individuals want to gain from these experiences.

- Phase 2: Attend professional development activities with the primary focus aligned to your objectives.
- Phase 3: Come together following activities to determine what was learned that should be implemented in the school to increase student achievement; collectively plan how this implementation can occur; assign responsibilities and timelines; and determine what outcomes will indicate success for students.

- Understand that change is difficult yet pervasive in most organizations. New ways of thinking are critical to achieve the change desired.

SHARED PERSONAL PRACTICE

Collaborate with others to ensure the success of all children.

As you move through the revolving door, it is important that everyone else seeking the same goal collaborate in accomplishing it. Those individuals in front of you, you and your party, and those coming behind you must all act in concert to move through the door without experiencing major problems. It is not enough for you to do the right thing; everyone involved must act purposefully if the goal is to be accomplished. If someone tries to go too fast or does not bring his or her baggage along at the appropriate speed, everyone gets stuck! Moving everyone through the door in a timely fashion and with all of their belongings takes collaboration, cooperation, and a consistent eye on your vision.

The need for collaboration and coordination from everyone is essential for sustaining the hard won achievements of a PLC. Everyone in the school is mutually dependent on everyone else in the school. What any one person or group does affects the accomplishments of the others. Recognizing and working with this is critical to sustaining a PLC in the school or district.

Huffman, Pankake, and Muñoz (2006) gave Fullan's (2005) concept of lateral and vertical accountability meaning when they described Mineral Springs Independent School District in their case story (see Chapter 9). It is not enough for the language arts teachers to work long and hard at collaborating if the math teachers do not parallel these efforts. It is important for teachers to work collaboratively and the administrative team to be supportive of those efforts.

This extends outside the campus as well. Schools can succeed in creating PLCs, but if the feeder schools or the district leadership team does not provide the necessary support for sustaining and even increasing the gains made, campus achievements will quickly become undone. Individual units within the school should work collectively, but it is equally important that in the larger context of the school, other schools, and the district as a whole, must create the conditions necessary for sustainability.

The following actions can help incorporate shared personal practice in your school:

- Arrange for staff to observe each other throughout the school day.
- Create opportunities for staff to come together to discuss their work, to review student work, and provide feedback.
- Ensure that follow-up and coaching are elements of all professional development activities in the school.
- Collaboratively plan professional development activities that address the needs of the school as a whole, as well as the separate teaching units.
- Capitalize on the expertise of in-house resources.
- Build a sense of collective efficacy within the school by such actions as creating situations where faculty are interdependent or celebrate successes of content groups, grade levels, or teams.
- Utilize central office content specialists in the development and implementation of best practices for teaching students.
- Invite representatives from feeder schools to planning meetings and professional development events.
- Encourage and actively participate in vertical teaming at the district level.

SUPPORTIVE CONDITIONS—STRUCTURES

Maintain the structures that exist and create new ones as needed.

Anyone who has who has been traveling for a while will recall that the time when these revolving doors that accommodate you and your luggage has not always existed. In fact you may recall or even still experience trying to get yourself and your luggage through a single, narrow stationary door. This required shifting items about to free a hand for pushing or pulling the door open and then quickly trying to move you and your items through before the door closed on you and your belongings. Depending on what you were hauling, you may or may not make it through the door on your first attempt. Fortunately most of these original doors have been replaced with the more convenient, hands-free models that more efficiently facilitate the task.

Most likely, old structures will be replaced by newer ones as you move toward establishing a PLC in your school. For instance, schedules may have changed to allow more opportunities for teachers and administrators to work collaboratively. Or perhaps subject-area or grade-level organizations have been changed to better address the instructional needs of students and include mixed groups to facilitate whole school change. It may be that new systems for decision making, recommendations, and input have been formulated to ensure more comprehensive and transparent communications. No doubt, there have been countless structures created, modified, and discarded in order to seek alignment and provide support for achieving the mission and vision of the school as a PLC. In order to sustain the progress made, these new structures need to be maintained and adapted.

The following steps will help ensure that structures are maintained and adapted when needed:

- Conduct small group or focus sessions with faculty and staff to assess how structures are working and make modifications as needed.
- Involve those closest to implementation in conversations regarding suggested structural changes needed when new ideas for action are being considered.
- Explain in handbooks or other documents the specific steps for decision making, information gathering, and communication processes. Edit these documents as agreed-upon changes are made.
- Establish a monitoring system that enables you to know constantly what is happening in all facets of the school's operations.
- Apply business process mapping, benchmarking, and other total quality management tools in identifying the efficiency and effectiveness of current practices

SUPPORTIVE CONDITIONS—RELATIONSHIPS

Pay attention to the people in your organization.

Moving through these doors smoothly requires that you pay attention, not only to your own movement, but also to the progress of others. If someone has never operated a door like this you may need to provide some coaching to assist him or her; for others you may provide additional information. Ultimately, you may need to make a quick assessment of whether it is time for you to proceed or allow others to go first. You may even find yourself stuck, only to find someone ready to coach you through the door. To successfully maneuver through the door you should be mindful of others seeking the same goal, which often requires adjusting your own actions to achieve the goals of those around you.

If paying attention to others is required to achieve such a minor goal as opening a revolving door, obviously it will be essential if the work you have done in fostering a PLC is to be sustained. The very essence of a PLC involves purposeful considerations in developing the relationships among the adults in the organization. You must take the initiative in nurturing, coaching, and rewarding adults as they work together for the benefit of student learning.

The following behaviors promote supportive conditions that foster relationships:

- Initiate social interaction opportunities (e.g., professional development, celebrations, and team planning sessions) that allow individuals to get to know one another at a deeper, more personal level. This develops trust and promotes respect.
- Delegate effectively to ensure clarity of authority and responsibility, focus on results not processes, and reduce conflict and confusion between administrators and teachers and among teachers themselves.
- Listen to one another and value differing voices. Utilize several venues (i.e., before school, after school, at lunch or planning time, during coffee and conversation sessions or team and committee meetings).
- Engage people in dialogue to resolve chronic problems that continue to arise.
- Encourage people to explore their mental models and remain open to other opinions.

SUPPORTIVE CONDITIONS—EXTERNAL SUPPORT SYSTEMS

Access and generate support from the larger external context.

Continuing with our metaphor, the operation of the revolving door most directly involves those in the process of moving through it. This does not, however, mean that those individuals are the only ones connected to this effort. Other individuals inside have plans to go out, individuals outside are waiting their turn to come in, and there is an entire cast of individuals unseen that have designed and built the door, maintained it to keep it working, and helped keep things operating with the other structures and services of the hotel or airport.

This is also true for the individual school operating as a PLC. Parents, central office personnel, and state officials have their own responsibilities that ensure the larger context in which the school exists operates smoothly. They are also present to assist when the school staff needs help.

Parents support their children by providing basic needs and support for the school's activities in a variety of ways. Similarly, central office personnel support schools in numerous disparate ways. They do everything from making sure that the busses run every day to providing instructional assistance and support and ensuring that policies are adopted and implemented that ensure the district is operating legally, ethically, and efficiently.

Though we sometimes complain about the state's requirements for schools, it is still the case that education is a state function, and thus it is incumbent on state officials to provide guidance and resources and to monitor what is occurring in the individual districts through funding, rules and regulations for operations, and accountability to the taxpayers they serve. These external, sometimes unseen, individuals and organizations work to sustain the system of which each school is a part.

We all know what disruptions can occur when these external entities do not function properly. On the other hand, we often take them for granted when they operate appropriately. Schools desiring to maintain their successful efforts in creating a PLC must not take these external entities for granted. Rather, purposeful attention to and involvement of each should be pursued. The state, the district, and the school working in concert to reach the school's vision is one of the most powerful ways to systemically sustain reform.

Implementation may involve the following actions that engage external individuals and entities:

- Include critical components of PLC sustainability in the school improvement plan and request opportunities to present that plan for approval to the Board of Education to increase awareness and gain support for your efforts.
- Invite central office specialists to visit with staff regarding services and materials available to assist with curriculum and instruction.
- Communicate with individuals at the district or state office and ask questions about possible services and resources.
- Be sure you are on the mailing list for state department newsletters or bulletins. This will ensure that you know what is expected and you will not miss any opportunities for grants or staff development funding.
- Involve parents and community members in various task forces, site committees, and planning groups operating in the school.
- Create periodic appreciation activities for parents and community members to acknowledge their efforts and encourage their continuous involvement.
- Create a school foundation to allow benefactors to assist the school with donations that can be used to help students with basic needs or perhaps scholarships for post-secondary education.

SUSTAINABILITY IS POSSIBLE

The image of the revolving door may be simple, but it is easy to imagine for most everyone in the school—even the students. Sometimes it is the simple idea that can help us understand what is complex. According to Morgan (2006), "The use of metaphor implies *a way of thinking* and *a way of seeing* that pervade how we understand our world generally. . . . We use metaphor whenever we attempt to understand one element of experience in terms of another" (p. 4). In his book, *Images of Organization*, Morgan uses metaphors to assist leaders in seeing their organizations in new ways.

According to Hargreaves and Fink (2003), educational change is "rarely easy, always hard to justify, and almost impossible to sustain" (p. 693). The revolving door metaphor has been created to help you view the process of sustaining a PLC as something familiar, something doable, something necessary. Although sustaining a school's PLC is significantly more complex than moving through the revolving door, it is possible if leaders can mobilize and maintain efforts toward achieving the vision. All of the good work of staff, students, parents, and administrators, in developing and implementing a PLC, will fade like so many other change efforts without a systematic plan to sustain its success.

Sustaining a PLC is not simple, but engaging in each step needed to accomplish it is achievable with a unified vision, shared leadership, and knowledge and skills. Just as you use your knowledge and skills to take each step and necessary action to move you and others through that revolving door successfully, take what you have learned in your journey of creating and implementing the PLC to guide you in sustaining it. Use the concepts and tools presented in this book to help everyone in the school

- make sure that the vision is always on the horizon.
- embed leadership as a quality in the organization, not just in individuals.
- collaborate with others to ensure the success of all children.
- learn and work together in new ways—create and innovate.
- provide support for communicating and learning.
- pay attention to the people in your organization by valuing and nurturing excellence.
- access and generate support from the larger external context.

Put into practice some of the specific suggestions following each of these actions and engage in *best practices*. But go beyond them; create actions that best fit your situation and take action both individually and collectively. Without purposeful and coordinated action you will get results, but not the results you want.

Sustainability requires that you collectively get through the door and address what you find on the other side. There will always be new opportunities on the horizon, problems to solve, resources to utilize, and knowledge to use. Collectively, we can never rest on our laurels or we will surely regress. The unknown should excite and stimulate creative thinking and action. Much like acknowledging the proverbial elephant, we must view the whole system and work together to achieve the vision. When like-minded people are passionate and committed to student learning, they exhibit a strong sense of collective efficacy. As one superintendent expressed regarding a seemingly overwhelming situation, "Yes, it is difficult, but not impossible" (Valle, 2008).

12

Final Reflections

Moving Schools Forward

Kristine Kiefer Hipp and Jane Bumpers Huffman

As we look back on the closing of our last book, *Reculturing Schools as Professional Learning Communities*, we are encouraged with the significant advances made toward creating and sustaining PLCs in diverse contexts.

In 2003, we posed a challenge and quoted the words of Rosa Parks, whose message continues to inspire confidence and hope in believers. "The challenge for school leaders in this millennium is to guide their school communities from concept to capability—a capability that is self-sustaining and that will institutionalize reform" (Huffman & Hipp, p. 150).

> We are not where we want to be, We are not where we are going to be, But, we are not where we were.
>
> —Rosa Parks

Specifically, the challenge for school leaders was to move well-intentioned efforts toward initiating and implementing PLCs to sustainability (i.e., continuous learning and best practices embedded in the school culture). Writers, such as Shirley Hord, Michael Fullan, Andy Hargreaves, Dean Fink, Alan Blankstein, Ron Heifetz, Marty Linsky, and numerous other scholars and practitioners, have guided and reinforced our research and practice. In 2009, we remain believers.

We believe the phrase *concept to capability* is more achievable now than ever before, and that sustainable efforts are within our grasp if we work purposefully for intentional learning for professionals and students. In schools that are value added, which demonstrate increasing student results year after year, teachers and administrators are focused on growth and innovation; they grow change in their schools organically and integrate creative ways of thinking and experimenting.

As Ms. Parks believed, the achievement of the dream is ahead of us, and if educators in schools can work as a united force, with an undeviating focus on collective learning for students and staff, we can assuredly reach our vision. As professionals, we can settle for nothing less.

From our research and experience, our work with schools and districts, presentations with colleagues nationally and cross-continents, and writing, we have revealed critical information that challenges us to think in new ways. We are convinced that dialogue focused on shared goals is the key to progress, that supportive conditions in schools are imperative to facilitate collective learning, and that attention needs to shift to the human side of change, that is, developing relationships that ultimately make everything possible.

We have witnessed a shift in attention from management to leadership that builds on individual and collective strengths and that addresses student outcomes first. This shift comes from developing knowledge and skill in facilitating change, which engages the entire system around student and professional learning. Similar to our last book, our intent is to bring clarity, substance, and structure to the PLC concept and to provide examples, tools, and strategies related to people working together interdependently toward a common vision.

We repeat, as Davis maintained in 2002, the notion that community development is not an achievement or event, it is an *undertaking*. We concur that such an "undertaking requires resources, leadership, and continuous support to succeed and be meaningful throughout the entire school community" (Huffman & Hipp, 2003, p. 149). Therefore, school leaders must establish conditions that encourage new ways of thinking and interacting to build capacity and school-wide commitment based on shared values. With vision and leadership, supported by resources, interdependent thinking will evolve so all people are connected and valued, and students achieve their potential.

OVERVIEW OF BOOK

A primary purpose of this book was to demystify the concept of a PLC. Our definition describes the professionals in the school as they work collectively and purposefully to create and sustain an instructional culture for all students and adults. We shared the results twelve years of experiences as we worked intentionally with school personnel who were intentional about developing learning communities.

In our work with these schools, we found there is hope for educators as they struggle to create cultures that make a difference for students. A sense of hope emerged as we listened to the voices of administrators and teachers who collaborated to understand the PLC concept and to design programs and strategies that develop leadership capacity and provide meaningful results.

Another result of our work was to design and share PLC tools that assist educators in defining, operationalizing, and assessing schools and staff related to the PLC model. To help educators in their work, we provided informal and formal tools including the

- PLCO
- PLCA-R
- PLC-ICM
- ESS-ICM
- PLCDR
- TEBS-C
- Initial Plan for Creating PLCs

In addition we included the PTLC, a school strategy that addresses, at the classroom level, a process for teaching, learning, and accountability. A descriptive vignette and a visual of the PTLC are also offered that give a clear picture of that model's implementation and the steps involved.

An important feature of our book includes three case stories that personalize and reveal the challenges and successes of diverse schools. This information assists practitioners to apply what they have learned as they are challenged daily with serious issues that impact learning. In Chapter 11 we focused on sustainability in schools using a metaphorical approach to simulate a real-life experience.

This final chapter presents a summary of insights and the challenges that continue to frame our work in the future. Through our work in schools we have identified serious challenges in the following areas:

- Leadership succession
- Collective efficacy
- Urban issues of race and class
- High school reform
- Expanding leadership capacity
- Technical and adaptive change

These challenges present areas that educators, parents, community members, and policy makers will deal with over the next decade.

CONCLUDING INSIGHTS

As a result of our work with educators, we uncovered and thus highlight several insights related to PLC development in the following areas:

- The relevancy of PLCs.
- Continuous learning.
- Supportive conditions.
- Connections among leadership.
- Collective efficacy and PLCs.
- Inclusive leadership.
- Involvement of all stakeholders.

We also know that efforts must be intentionally focused on student achievement that is guided by data. The use of data should be precise and focused on the needs of each student (Fullan, Hill, & Crévola, 2006).

We believe that to maximize efforts, continuous learning related to vision and goals reviewed regularly and consistently will provide lateral and vertical accountability to meet the needs of all students. In *Reculturing Schools as Professional Learning Communities* (2003), we asserted that:

> to meet the diverse needs of students, people must change their attitudes and habits of action; thus change involves learning. This requires a capacity to continuously learn and adapt to a variety of complex environments.

Thus, teachers and administrators collaborating at all levels on purposeful tasks related to student achievement will ensure the best chance for student success.

Another insight focuses on the support practitioners receive as they learn and collaborate in new ways. Professional support is ongoing and includes: development of strong and trusting interactions, time to pursue learning, and reinforcement for meeting students' needs in a safe and risk-free environment. Throughout our research and fieldwork, we continue to find that supportive conditions, such as trust, respect, and inclusiveness, remain the glue that allows effective communication, learning, and growth to occur.

We also recognize that the varying connections including perceived leadership capacity, collective efficacy, student achievement, and PLCs are strongly related (Mawhinney, Haas, & Wood, 2005; Olivier & Hipp, 2006) and worthy of extensive study. By encouraging teachers to reach their potential and make a positive impact, leaders not only provide opportunities and needed support and resources, but also assist in developing a strong teacher leadership base needed for the school improvement process. For instance, teachers facilitate work in small groups around issues of teaching and learning and initiate whole school change (Hipp, 2004).

Creating dynamic schools where leadership is broad and inclusive is imperative. Schools involved in purposeful efforts, which broaden leadership that includes teachers and administrators, define shared vision based on a focus on student learning, and reflect a culture of continual support and creativity. These characteristics increase the probability that schools reflecting this image will make great strides in becoming learning organizations that address critical student needs and provide learning opportunities for all.

Our final insight recognizes the importance of involving all stakeholders. Although we believe the professionals in the school provide the first line of *community* for the students; we also believe that involving central office instructional staff, parents, and community members strengthens and extends the impact for students. Accordingly, when administrators and teachers interact with the external support systems and collaborate within a common agenda, improvement increases and becomes embedded in an inclusive culture.

Taking this idea one step further, Fullan (2004) proposes the tri-level model that includes schools, central office, and state working together for systemic reform. In this model all three groups work toward common goals with focus, commitment, and structure. Fullan suggests, "We need more examples where entire systems are actively engaged in tri-level reform—where the criterion of success is large-scale engagement and development of all three levels, with the outcome being continuous improvement through raising the bar and closing the gap of student performance" (p. 16).

REMAINING CHALLENGES

As Chapter 2 indicates, our PLC work began with a federally funded project in 1998, *Creating Continuous Communities of Inquiry and Improvement* through SEDL in Austin under Shirley Hord, manager for SEDL's Strategies for Increasing School Success initiative. At the completion of the grant in 2000, several authors from this book continued to work collaboratively with one end in mind: how to create instructional cultures that advance student learning.

In the process of learning about the PLC concept, our goal continues to be to promote this instructional culture with rigor and integrity. This work is not easy!

We also support PLCs as the *promise* of educational reform, as others claim, a belief reinforced by our findings. However, several challenges remain if PLCs are to be implemented widely.

Leadership Succession

Principals come and go without strategic plans for succession that prepare leaders to take their place. At times leaders who are ill-equipped to lead in a PLC culture are named. We are aware that principals often move into new schools and ignore the existing culture; rather they move forward without input or without capitalizing on the expertise and influence of their staff.

These regrettable scenarios could be avoided if principals and central office personnel would design a leadership succession plan that provides for a seamless transition and increases the chance that change would occur as intended. The sustainability of progress is compromised because input, involvement, and ownership are absent.

If relationships exist between perceived leadership capacity and collective efficacy in mature, value-added PLCs, it behooves administrators to intentionally prepare leaders with appropriate knowledge, skills, and attitudes to transition into these roles when opportunities arise. Moreover, teachers in schools who enjoy a strong sense of personal and collective efficacy would be more apt to show confidence in assuming these positions.

Collective Efficacy

Since the 1977 Rand Study by Berman and McLaughlin teacher efficacy, a teacher's belief in the educability of students, has been recognized for its impact on several factors related to school improvement. Although this construct has materialized through several iterations and measures, we continue to be encouraged with connections among factors found in maturing PLCs.

In maturing PLCs, leadership capacity is intentionally developed and nurtured; teachers believe that, together, they can impact student learning, and this becomes apparent as they continuously show evidence of increased student learning. The power of collective efficacy, an emerging area of study, is worthy of further attention; as individuals, if we believe we can accomplish something together, we often find we can and do.

We tend to increase those odds when the majority of the people in an organization work without fear and with confidence and unity to achieve common goals.

Urban Issues of Race and Class

Urban issues permeate the media on a daily basis and pose significant challenges for our schools. Students continue to fail despite substantial dollars and efforts targeting school reform. Hipp and her colleagues participated in a Wallace Foundation grant that was the impetus for 18 individually written case stories by K–8 principals from two urban districts over a period of 3 years resulting in two books (Wallace Fellows, 2007, 2008). These principals met regularly and worked collaboratively on common issues, building lateral capacity across school districts, while deepening their understanding of the importance of PLCs in sustaining student achievement (Hipp & Weber, 2008).

The principals identified three emerging themes that separate urban contexts from other school contexts: magnitude, urgency, and complexity. Briefly defined, they view magnitude in relation to size and scope; urgency parallels immediacy; and complexity addresses the interrelated parts of the system that cannot be understood separately. All three themes are imperative in meeting the unique needs of urban students.

The effects of classism, which include poverty issues, are not only confined to urban education, but are also reflected in countless rural districts as well. Issues of race and class are abundant and have become the primary focus of educational reform. Since *A Nation at Risk* (1983) and the landmark books authored by Jonathan Kozol (1991) and Alfie Kohn (1999), economic and social activists have persisted in their cause to replace doubt with action in closing the achievement gap.

We join numerous researchers (Childress, Elmore, & Grossman, 2006; Cuban & Usdan, 2003; Darling-Hammond, 2004; Delpit, 1996; Giles, Johnson, Brooks, & Jacobson, 2005; Hilliard, 2004; Meier, Kohn, Darling-Hammond, Sizer, & Wood, 2004; Noguera, 2003; Payne, 2005; Sharratt & Fullan, 2006) in this quest for moral purpose.

We urge leaders to continue to adapt to environmental realities and consider how the PLC dimensions could impact the issues surrounding magnitude, urgency, and complexity if approached purposefully and assertively to address urban school reform. This is particular important in lieu of the compelling statistics that reflect the crisis in high school education.

High School Reform

It is unarguable that school reform continues to pose a challenge for high schools, particularly those situated in urban settings. In our continuing facilitation and research involving a second Wallace grant (Weber & Hipp, 2008), it was obvious that our efforts needed to address the chronic and significant issues facing high school. Thus, we are now partnering with the state, universities, and school district high school leadership teams to advance the state of Wisconsin's aligned system of leadership incorporating these three initiatives:

- Standards that address changes to policies and practices.
- Training for leadership team development at the site level and through a statewide network.
- Conditions that identify and assess leadership development and expectations at all levels—preservice through the master level.

Fourteen comprehensive high schools in five urban districts were chosen for our current work for several reasons. There is a lack of evidence in the literature and in schools related to how PLCs affect high school reform issues. Moreover, high schools have the largest achievement gap between students of color and white students. The size and complexity of high schools raise significant leadership challenges; therefore, the position of the high school principal typically attracts the fewest applicants.

Structural and cultural reforms have done little to transform the reconfiguration of schools and make the leadership role of the principal even more complex. Finally, high school principals are often promoted from other leadership positions, and fall through gaps in induction systems that support principals in their initial placements.

The intent of the Wallace high school grant is to augment the strengths of the current system, address the achievement gaps in Wisconsin's five urban districts, and adapt to changes in the environment to add to the *best practices* found by other researchers across the continent that confront these chronic problems. If leaders are to be successful in addressing these issues, then it will require developing leadership capacity across all schools and school districts.

Leadership Capacity

Without question, we believe expanding leadership capacity is key. To move teachers to such a belief, school leaders need to understand schools are part of a larger complex adaptive system that includes the district, community, and state. Principals need to be competent in facilitating change among seemingly disparate parts, distinct personalities and styles, and at times, opposing priorities for a common goal. Principals need to model passion, integrity, and commitment to inspire others to expand leadership capacity and assume new roles and responsibilities.

"Leadership would be a safe undertaking if your organizations and communities only faced problems for which they already knew the solutions" (Heifetz & Linsky, 2002, p. 13). This assertion poses the need for understanding the differences between technical and adaptive problems that require different approaches to change.

Technical and Adaptive Change

For years leaders have applied technical solutions to adaptive problems to little avail. Technical problems require technical solutions that are already in our grasp. Within the organization there are those who possess the knowledge and skills to provide adequate solutions. However, the difficulty often lies with adaptive problems that cannot be solved with existing resources because they require systems thinking, innovation, and new ways of thinking.

Without a desire to learn in community, which is the foundation of the PLC, it is impossible to change the culture of an organization's values, attitudes, and assumptions (Deal & Peterson, 1999). Heifetz and Linsky (2002) maintain, "The sustainability of change depends on having the people with the problem internalize the change itself" (p. 13).

Leaders need to distinguish between technical and adaptive change to effectively facilitate appropriate solutions to problems that continue to persist, perhaps the greatest challenge leaders face. Understanding the conditions that exist determine the strategy used. If we continually pursue the wrong strategies, we lose the confidence of our people, as well as their commitment and energy.

School leadership that addresses adaptive problems applies strategies and practices that promote organizational change and develops the adaptability to thrive in complex and demanding conditions. Leadership involves what people do to mobilize others in organizations and communities to do adaptive work. Our Canadian colleagues, Mitchell and Sackney (2000), who have contributed significantly to school improvement worldwide through their research on learning organizations in general, assert:

> Profound improvement happens from within, from a deep internal search for meaning, relevance, and connection. It is a search for those things that will make one's life more authentic and purposeful, and it emerges naturally when one sees a new destination and then sets out on the journey. (p. 139)

SUMMARY

We have reason to believe that several schools are successfully implementing and are also beginning to see evidence of sustaining the PLC process. The following are but two examples of schools and districts becoming, implementing, and sustaining PLC efforts in the United States. We also acknowledge that leaders in other countries are also achieving similar results through intentional efforts related to building learning cultures.

A principal in a Title I elementary school that has 27 languages spoken among its student population says,

> The biggest impact working on becoming a PLC has been in the sharing of data, teaching strategies, and interventions for individual students. Teachers meet at least twice and sometimes three times a week to plan lessons, look at recent local assessment data, discuss interventions for struggling students, and share teaching strategies.

She comments about sharing leadership, "As a principal I am working toward building leadership capacity in my staff. I feel our impact can be more powerful if we encourage everyone in the school to contribute and make decisions" (personal correspondence with Kim Scoggins).

From the district perspective, an associate superintendent explains how schools in his district have gone about developing PLCs. "Both high schools have studied the work of Dr. Shirley Hord and experienced several levels of training in developing PLCs. They have utilized the PLC framework and philosophy to address critical issues such as student achievement in the areas of math and science, levels of intervention for at-risk students, and the development and implementation of comprehensive strategic plans."

He also describes other campuses that operationalize the PLC dimensions without any formal training. "These leaders build the ideas of a PLC into the culture and fabric of the school community. The principals develop learning goals that support the shared vision and collaboratively explore with the teachers what they need to learn. Teachers develop learning cadres and self-select topics to investigate. Principals provide support for these activities through scheduling, providing proximate work spaces, and through release time teachers can engage in professional learning and dialogue" (personal correspondence with John Doughney).

As detailed by these two school leaders, successes are occurring in schools and districts as a result of principals developing leadership capacity, teachers collaboratively planning, and principals and central office personnel providing the supports needed for teachers to interact and achieve results with their students.

Yet, Fullan (2005) reminds us, "Sustainability is the capacity of a system to engage in the complexities of continuous improvement consistent with deep values of human purpose" (p. ix). Therefore, principal leaders, who facilitate systems change, must also be intentional and skillful in promoting individual, interpersonal, and organizational capacity building within the system *to enhance moral purpose.*

In addition, we concur with Davidovich, Nikolay, Laugerman, and Commodore (2010) that improvement is not enough, that it is insufficient without innovation. This requires school leaders to see clearly that schools reflect the ever-changing environment and recognize that disturbances and uncertainties are constant and call for thinking in new ways. Moreover, in her work on complex adaptive systems, Margaret Wheatley (personal communication) asserts, "A stable organization is a dying organization." Leaders must become comfortable with these disturbances and uncertainties as a natural part of the change process.

One essential strategy in balancing this roller-coaster ride to sustaining healthy cultures is to cultivate the development of relationships among all stakeholders. Strong relationships provide alignment at all levels, communication opportunities and the connections needed in times of change and challenge. "When conditions of sustainability are put in place, the work is more efficient, effective, and rewarding. . . . People find meaning by connecting to others; and they find well-being by making progress on problems important to their peers and of benefit beyond themselves" (Fullan, 2005, p. 104).

Finally, we continue to believe that transformational principals can make a difference in student learning by influencing internal school processes, providing support, and engaging teachers to participate in meaningful decision making, and developing a shared sense of responsibility (Huffman & Hipp, 2003).

The principal is the key player in school reform. The leadership (or lack of leadership) the principal provides sets the tone and the pace for the efforts of all the stakeholders affecting students' lives. We believe that with strong principal leadership, school personnel can work and think together in new ways of communicating, organizing, and reflecting to create adaptive systems that provide students with opportunities to achieve their best.

Notes

NOTE FOR CHAPTER 4

1. For development and validation procedures of the initial measure refer to Huffman and Hipp, Chapter 8, Assessing Schools as PLCs, 2003.

NOTE FOR CHAPTER 6

1. The process has been refined and is now described in the following publication: Cowan, D., Joyner, S., & Beckwith, S. (2008). *Working systemically in action: A guide for facilitators*. Austin: SEDL.

NOTE FOR CHAPTER 9

1. The Texas Essential Knowledge and Skills, or TEKS, are the Texas state standards.

References

Airasian, P. W. (2004). *Classroom assessment: Concepts and applications.* Boston: McGraw-Hill.

Andrews, D., & Lewis, M. (2004). Building sustainable futures: Emerging understandings of the significant contribution of the professional learning community. *Improving Schools, 7*(2), 129–150.

Aptekar, L. (1983). Mexican-American high school student's perception of school. *Adolescence, 18*(70), 345–357.

Argyris, C. (1990). *Overcoming organizational defenses.* Needham, MS: Allyn and Bacon.

Astuto, T. A., Clark, D. L., Read, A. M., McGree, K., & Fernandez, L. K. (1993). *Challenges to dominant assumptions controlling education reform.* Andover, MA: Regional Laboratory of the Educational Improvement of the Northeast and Island.

Bacon, L. (1994). *It's about time! A report from the National Education Association's Special Committee on time resources.* (ERIC Document Reproduction Service No. ED 4582000).

Badaracco, J. L. (2002). *Leading quietly: An unorthodox guide to doing the right thing.* Boston: Harvard Business School Press.

Barth, R. S. (1990). *Improving schools from within.* San Francisco: Jossey-Bass.

Barth, R. S. (2006). *Improving relationships within the schoolhouse.* Educational Leadership, 63(6), 8-13.

Becker, H. J. (1987). *Addressing the needs of different groups of early adolescent: Effects of varying school and classroom organizational practices on students from different social backgrounds and abilities.* (Report No. 16.) Baltimore, MD: Center for Research on Elementary and Middle Schools, The John Hopkins University. (ERIC Document Reproduction Service No. ED291506).

Begley, P. T., & Johannson, O. (2000). *Using what we know about values: Promoting authentic leadership and democracy in schools.* Paper presented at the annual UCEA Conference, Albuquerque, New Mexico.

Berlin, B. M., & Cienkus, R. C. (1989). Size: The ultimate educational issue? *Education and Urban Society, 21*(2), 228–231.

Berman, P., & McLaughlin, M. W. (1977). *Federal programs supporting educational change.* Vol. VII: *Factors affecting implementation and continuation* (Report No. R-1589/7-HEW). Santa Monica, CA: The Rand Corporation.

Bernhardt, V. L. (2004). *Data analysis for continuous school improvement.* Larchmont, NY: Eye on Education, Inc.

Blankstein, A. M. (2004). *Failure is not an option: Six principles that guide student achievement in high-performing schools.* Thousand Oaks, CA: Corwin Press Inc.

Blankstein, A. M., Houston, P. D., & Cole, R. W. (2007). *Sustaining professional learning communities.* Thousand Oaks, CA: Corwin Press.

Block, P. (1996). *Stewardship.* San Francisco: Berrett-Koehler Publishers, Inc.

Bohm, D. (1996). *On dialogue.* London: Routledge.

Borg, W. R., & Gall, M. D. (1983). *Educational research.* New York: Longman.

Boyd, V. (1992). *School context: Bridge or barriers to change?* Austin: Southwest Educational Development Laboratory.

Boyd, V., & Hord, S. M. (1994). Schools as learning communities. *Issues . . . about Change.* Austin: Southwest Educational Development Laboratory.

Brewer, H. (2001). Ten steps to success. *Journal of Staff Development, 22*(1), 30–31.

Brown, D. F. (1995). Experiencing shared leadership: Teachers' reflections. *Journal of School Leadership, 5*(4), 334–355.

Bryk, A. S., Easton, J. Q., Kerbrew, D., Rollow, S. G., & Sebring, P. A. (1994). The state of Chicago school reform. *Phi Delta Kappan, 76*(1), 74–78.

Bryk, A., & Schneider, B. (2003). Trust in schools: A core resource for school reform. *Educational Leadership, 60*(6), 40–45.

Burns, J. M. (1979). *Leadership.* New York: Harper & Row Publishers.

Bushman, J. (2006). Teachers as walk-through partners. *Educational Leadership, 63*(6), 58–61.

Cawelti, G. (2004). A synthesis of research on high-performing school systems. In G. Cawelti (Ed.), *Handbook of research on improving student achievement* (3rd ed., pp. 10–24). Arlington, VA: Educational Research Service.

Childress, S., Elmore, R., & Grossman, A. (2006, November). How to manage urban school districts. *Harvard Business Review,* 55.

Cotton, K. (2003). *Principals and student achievement: What the research says.* Alexandria, VA: Association of Supervision and Curriculum Development.

Covey, S. (2004). *The seven habits of highly effective people.* New York: Free Press.

Cowan, D. F. (2006). Creating learning communities in low-performing sites: A systemic approach to alignment. *Journal of School Leadership, 16*(5), 596–610.

Cowan, D., & Hord, S. M. (1999). *Reflections on school renewal and communities of continuous inquiry and improvement.* Paper presented at the annual meeting of the American Educational Research Association, Montreal, Canada.

Cowan, D., Joyner, S., & Beckwith, S. (2008). *Working systemically in action: A guide for facilitators.* Austin, TX: Southwest Educational Development Laborator.

Cowan, D. F. (2003). The PLC connection to school improvement. In J. B. Huffman & K. K. Hipp (Eds.), *Reculturing schools as professional learning communities* (pp. 75-82). Lanham, MD: Scarecrow Education.

Creighton, T. B. (2001). Data analysis in administrators' hands: An oxymoron? *The*

School Administrator, 58(4), 6–11.

Crowther, F., Kaagan, S., Ferguson, M. & Hahn, L. (2002). *Developing teacher leaders: How teacher leadership enhances school success.* Thousand Oaks, CA: Corwin Press.

Cuban, L., & Usdan, M. (2003). *Powerful reforms with shallow roots: Improving America's urban schools.* New York: Teachers College Press.

Daresh, J. (2002). *What it means to be a principal.* Thousand Oaks, CA: Corwin Press, Inc.

Darling-Hammond, L. (1990). Teacher professionalism: Why and how. In A. Lieberman (Ed.), *Schools as collaborative cultures* (pp. 25–50). Bristol, PA: Flamer Press.

―――. (2004). Conclusion: Schools that work for all children. In C. Glickman (Ed.), *Letters to the next president* (pp. 239–253). New York: Teachers College Press.

Datnow, A. (2005). The sustainability of comprehensive school reform models in changing district and state contexts. *Educational Administration Quarterly, 41*(1), 121–153.

Davidovich, B., Nikolay, P., Laugerman, B., & Commodore, C. (2010). *Beyond school improvement: The journey to innovative leadership.* Thousand Oaks, CA: Corwin Press.

Davidson, B. M., & Dell, G. L. (1996). *Transforming teachers' work: The impact of two principals' leadership styles.* Paper presented at the annual meeting of the American Educational Research Association, New York.

Deal, T. E., & Peterson, K. D. (1999). *Shaping school culture: The heart of leadership.* San Francisco: Jossey-Bass.

Delpit, L. (1996). Other people's children: Cultural conflict in the classroom. New York: Free Press.

Dewey, J. (1938). *Experience and education.* New York: MacMillan.

DuFour, R., DuFour, R., & Eaker, R. (2008). *Revisiting professional learning communities at work.* Bloomington, IN: Solution Tree.

DuFour, R., DuFour, R., Eaker, R., & Karhanek, G. (2004). *Whatever it takes: How professional learning communities respond when kids don't learn.* Bloomington, IN: National Educational Service.

DuFour, R., & Eaker, R. (1998). *Professional learning communities at work: Best practices for enhancing student achievement.* Bloomington, IN: National Educational Service.

DuFour, R., Eaker, R., & DuFour, R. (2005). *On common ground: The power of professional learning communities.* Bloomington, IN: Solution Tree.

Dunne, F., & Honts, F. (1998). *That group really makes me think! Critical friends groups and the development of reflective practitioners.* Paper presented at the annual meeting of the American Educational Research Association, San Diego.

Eaker, R., DuFour, R., & Burnette, R. (2002). *Getting started: Reculturing schools to become professional learning communities.* Bloomington, IN: National Educational Service.

Farkas, S., Johnson, J., & Duffett, A. (2003). *Rolling up their sleeves: Superintendents and principals about what's needed to fix public schools.* New York: Public Agenda.

Firestone, W. A. (1996). Images of teaching and proposals for reform: A comparison of ideas from cognitive and organizational research. *Educational Administration Quarterly, 32*(2), 209–235.

Foster, R., & Studdards, C. (1999). *Leadership within high school communities: A multiple study perspective.* Paper presented at the annual meeting of the American Educational Research Association, Montreal, Canada.

Freire, P. (1970). *Pedagogy of the oppressed.* New York: Herder & Herder.

Fullan, M. (1985). Change processes and strategies at the local level. *Elementary School Journal, 84*(3), 391–420.

———. (1993). *Change forces: Probing the depth of educational reform.* New York: Falmer Press.

———. (1995). The school as a learning organization: Distant dreams. *Theory into Practice, 34*(4), 230–235.

———. (2000). The three stories of education reform. *Phi Delta Kappan, 81*(8), 581–584.

———. (2001). *The new meaning of educational change* (3rd ed.). New York: Teachers College Press.

———. (2002). *Leadership in a culture of change.* San Francisco: Jossey-Bass.

———. (2003). *The moral imperative of school leadership.* Thousand Oaks, CA: Corwin Press, Inc.

———. (2004, Winter). Leadership across the system. *INSIGHT* (pp. 14–16).

———. (2005). *Leadership and sustainability: System thinkers in action.* Thousand Oaks, CA: Corwin Press, A Sage Publications Company.

———. (2006). Leading professional learning. *School Administrator, 63*(10), 10–14. Retrieved July 20, 2009, from http://findarticles.com/p/articles/mi_m0JSD/is_10_63/ai_n16865090/?tag=content;col1.

Fullan, M. (2007). *The new meaning of educational change.* New York: Teachers College Press.

Fullan, M., Hill, P., & Crévola, D. (2006). *Breakthrough.* Thousand Oaks, CA: Corwin Press.

Giles, C., Johnson, L., Brooks, S., & Jacobson, S. (2005). Building bridges, building community: Transformational leadership in a challenging urban context. *Journal of School Leadership, 15,* 519–545.

Glickman, C. D. (2002). *Leadership for learning.* Alexandria, VA: Association for Supervision and Curriculum Development.

Goals 2000: Educate America Act, Pub. L. no. 103-227, 20 U.S.C. et seq. 5811 (2004). Print

Goleman, D. (2006). *Social intelligence.* New York: Bantam Dell.

Gordon, S. (1991). *How to help beginning teachers succeed.* Alexandria, VA: Association for Supervision and Curriculum Development.

Guskey, T. R. (2000). *Evaluating professional development.* Thousand Oaks, CA: Corwin Press.

Guskey, T. R., & Peterson, K. D. (1993). The road to classroom change. *Educational Leadership, 53*(4), 10–14.

Hall, G. E., & Hord, S. M. (2006). *Implementing change: Patterns, principles and potholes* (2nd ed.). Boston: Allyn & Bacon.

Hargreaves, A. (1995, April). Renewal in the age of paradox. *Educational Leadership, 52*(7), 14–19.

Hargreaves, A., Earl, L., Moore, S., & Manning, S. (2001). *Learning to change: Teaching beyond subjects and standards.* San Francisco: Jossey-Bass.

Hargreaves, A., & Fink, D. (May 2003). Sustaining leadership. *Phi Delta Kappan, 84*(9), 693–700.

———. (2006). *Sustainable leadership*. San Francisco: Jossey-Bass.

Hart, A. W., & Murphy, M. J. (1990). New teacher react to redesigned teacher work. *American Journal of Education, 98*(3), 224–250.

Hawley, W. D., & Valli, L. (1999). The essentials of effective professional development: A new consensus. In L. Darling-Hammond and G. Skyes (Eds.), *Teaching as the learning professional* (pp. 127–150). San Francisco: Jossey-Bass.

Heifetz, R. A., & Linsky, M. (2002). *Leadership on the line*. Boston: Harvard Business School Press.

Henze, R., Katz, A., Norte, E., Sather, S. E., & Walker, E. (2002). *Leading for diversity: How leaders promote positive interethnic relations*. Thousand Oaks, CA: Corwin Press.

Hilliard, A. (2004). If we had the will to see it happen. In C. Glickman (Ed.), *Letters to the next president* (pp. 27–34). New York: Teachers College Press.

Hipp, K. A. (1997). *Documenting the effects of transformational leadership behavior on teacher efficacy*. Paper presented at the annual meeting of the American Educational Research Association, Chicago.

Hipp, K. A., & Huffman, J. B. (2002). *Documenting and examining practices in creating learning communities: Exemplars and non-exemplars*. Paper presented at the annual meeting of the American Educational Research Association, New Orleans.

Hipp, K. K., & Huffman, J. B. (2007). Using assessment tools as frames for dialogue to create and sustain professional learning communities. In L. Stoll & K. Seashore Louis (Eds.), *Professional learning communities: Divergence, depth and dilemmas*. New York: Teachers College Press.

Hipp, K. K. (2004, Spring/Summer). Teacher leadership: Illustrating practices reflective of schools engaged in purposeful efforts to create and sustain learning communities. *Leading & Managing: Journal of the Australian Council for Educational Leaders, 10*(2), 54–69.

Hipp, K. K., Huffman, J. B., Pankake, A. M., & Olivier, D. F. (June, 2008). Sustaining professional learning communities: Case studies. *Journal of Educational Change, 9*(2), 173-195.

Hipp, K. K., & Weber, P. (2008). Developing a professional learning community among urban school principals. *Journal of Urban Learning, Teaching and Research, 4*, 46–56.

Hoerr, T. R. (1996). Collegiality: A new way to define instructional leadership. *Phi Delta Kappan, 77*(5), 380–381.

Hollins, E. R. (2006). Transforming practice in urban schools. *Educational Leadership, 63*(6), 48–52.

Honzay, A. (1986–87). More is not necessarily better. *Educational Research Quarterly, 11*(2), 2–6.

Hord, S. M. (1997). *Professional learning communities: Communities of continuous inquiry and improvement*. Retrieved July 20, 2009, from Southwest Educational Development Laboratory at http://www.sedl.org/pubs/change34/welcome.html.

———. (1998). *School professional staff as learning community*. Austin, TX: Southwest Educational Development Laboratory.

————. (2004). *Learning together, leading together: Changing schools through professional learning communities.* New York: Teachers College Press.

Hord, S. M., & Hirsh, S. A. (2008). Making the promise a reality. In A. Blankstein, P. D. Houston, & R. W. Cole (Eds.), *Sustaining professional learning communities.* (pp. 23–40). Thousand Oaks, CA: Corwin Press.

Hord, S. M., & Sommers, W. A. (2008). *Leading professional learning communities: Voices from research and practice.* Thousand Oaks, CA: Corwin Press.

Hough, D. (March, 2005). The rise of the "elemiddle" school: Not every K–8 school applies best middle level practices. *School Administrator, 62*(3), 10.

Huffman, J. B. (2003). The role of shared values and vision in creating professional learning communities. *NASSP Bulletin, 87*(637), 21–34.

Huffman, J. B., Hipp, K. A., Pankake, A. M., & Moller, G. (2001). Professional learning communities: Leadership, integrated, vision-directed decision making and job embedded staff development. *Journal of School Leadership, 11*(5), 448–463.

Huffman, J. B., & Hipp, K. K. (2003). *Reculturing schools as professional learning communities.* Lanham, MD: Scarecrow Education.

Huffman, J. B., Pankake, A., & Muñoz, A. (2006). The tri-level model in actions: Site, district, and state plan for school accountability in increasing student success. *Journal of School Leadership, 16*(5), 569–582.

Huie, S. B., Buttram, J. L., Deviney, F. P., Murphy, K. M., & Ramos, M. A. (2004). *Alignment in SEDL's working systemically model.* Austin: Southwest Educational Development Laboratory.

Johnson, S. M. (1990). *Teachers at work: Achieving success in our schools.* New York: Basic Books.

————. (1996). *Leading to change.* San Francisco: Jossey-Bass.

Kannapel, P. J., & Clements, S. K. (2005). *Inside the black box of high performing high-poverty schools.* Lexington, KY: Prichard Committee for Academic Excellence.

Katzenmeyer, M., & Moller, G. (2001). *Awakening the sleeping giant: Leadership development for teachers* (2nd ed.). Thousand Oaks, CA: Corwin Press.

Kleine-Kracht, P. A. (1993). The principal in a community of learning. *Journal of School Leadership, 3*(4), 391–399.

Knapp, M. S. (2003). Professional development as a policy pathway. In R. E. Floden (Ed.), *Review of Research in Education* (pp. 109–157). Washington, DC: American Educational Research Association.

Kohn, A. (1999). *The schools our children deserve.* New York: Houghton Mifflin.

Kozol, J. (1991). *Savage inequalities: Children in America's schools.* New York: Crown Publisher, Inc.

LaFee, S. (2003). Professional learning communities. *School Administrator, 60*(5), 6–9, 11–12. Retrieved July 20, 2009, from http://findarticles.com/p/articles/mi_m0JSD/is_5_60/ai_101173943/?tag=content;col1.

Lakoff, G., & Johnson, M. (1980). *Metaphors we live by.* Chicago: University of Chicago Press.

Lambert, L. (1998a). *Building leadership capacity in schools.* Alexandria, VA: Association for Supervision and Curriculum Development.

————. (1998b). How to build leadership capacity. *Educational Leadership, 55*(7), 17–19.

————. (2003). *Leadership capacity for lasting school improvement.* Alexandria, VA: Association for Supervision and Curriculum Development.

Larsen, M. L., & Malen, B. (1997). *The elementary school principal's influence on teachers' curricular and instructional decisions.* Paper presented at the annual meeting of the American Educational Research Association, Chicago.

Leithwood, K., Leonard, L., & Sharratt, L. (1997). *Conditions fostering organizational learning in schools.* Paper presented at the annual meeting of the American Educational Research Association, San Francisco.

Lewis, A. C. (1989). *Restructuring America's schools.* Arlington, VA: American Association of School Administrators.

Lieberman, A., Falk, B., & Alexander, L. (1995). A culture in the making: Leadership in communities: *Ninety-fourth yearbook of the National Society for the Study of Education* (pp. 108–129). Chicago: University of Chicago Press.

Lieberman, A., & Miller, L. (1999). *Teachers — Transforming their world and their work.* Alexandra, VA: Association for Supervision and Curriculum Development.

Lindle, J. C. (1995/1996). Lessons from Kentucky about school-based decision making. *Educational Leadership, 35*(4), 20–23.

Little, J. W. (1997). *Excellence in professional development and professional community.* Washington, DC: Office of Educational Research and Improvement.

Louis, K. S., & Kruse, S. D. (1995). *Professionalism and community: Perspectives on reforming urban schools.* Thousand Oaks, CA: Corwin Press.

Louis, K. S., Kruse, S. D., & Marks, H. M. (1996). Schoolwide professional community. In F. Newmann and Associates (Eds.), *Authentic achievement: Restructuring schools for intellectual quality* (pp. 179–204). San Francisco: Jossey-Bass.

Louis, K. S., Toole, J., & Hargreaves, A. (1999). Rethinking school improvement. In J. Murphy & K. S. Louis (Eds.), *Handbook of research on educational administration* (2nd ed., pp. 251–276). San Francisco: Jossey-Bass.

Marzano, R. J. (2003). *What works in schools: Translating research into action.* Alexandria, VA: Association for Supervision and Curriculum Development.

Mason, S. (2003, April). *Learning from data: The role of professional learning communities.* A paper presented at the annual conference of the American Educational Research Association, Chicago. Retrieved July 22, 2009, from http://www.eric.ed.gov/ERICDocs/data/ericdocs2sql/content_storage_01/0000019b/80/1b/14/c0.pdf.

Mawhinney, H. B. (2004). Institutional effects of strategic efforts at community enrichment. *Journal of Educational Administration Quarterly, 30*(3), 324–341.

Mawhinney, H. B., Haas, J., & Wood, C. (November, 2005). *Teachers' perceptions of collective efficacy and school conditions for professional learning.* Paper presented to the Annual Meeting of the University Council for Educational Administration, Nashville.

McEwan, E. K. (2003). *Seven steps to effective instructional leadership.* Thousand Oaks, CA: Corwin Press.

McLaughlin, M. (1993). What matters most in teachers' workplace context. In J. W. Little & M. McLaughlin (Eds.), *Teacher's work: Individuals, colleagues, and context* (pp. 79–103). New York: Teachers College Press.

Meier, D., & Wood, G. (Eds.) (2004). *Many Children Left Behind.* Boston: Beacon Press.

Meier, D., Kohn, A., Darling-Hammond, L., Sizer, T., & Wood, G. (2004). *Many children left behind: How the No Child Left Behind Act is damaging our children and our schools.* Boston: BeaconPress.

Midgley, C., & Wood, S. (1993). Beyond site-based management: Empowering teachers to reform schools. *Phi Delta Kappan, 75*(3), 245–252.

Mitchell, C., & Sackney, L. (2000). *Profound improvement: Building capacity for a learning community.* Lisse, NL: Swets & Zeitlinger.

———. (2001, April). *Communities of leaders: Developing leadership capacity for a learning community.* Paper presented at the annual meeting of the American Educational Research Association, Seattle.

Mizell, H. (2003, April). *NCLB: Conspiracy, compliance, or creativity?* Remarks to the spring conference of the Maryland Council of Staff Developers. Retrieved July 20, 2009, from http://www.middleweb.com/HMnclb.html.

Moller, G., & Pankake, A. (2006). *Lead with me: A principal's guide to teacher leadership.* Larchmont, NY: Eye on Education.

Moore, S., & Shaw, P. (2000). *The professional learning needs and perceptions of secondary school teachers: Implications for a professional learning community.* Paper presented at the annual meeting of the American Educational Research Association, New Orleans.

Morgan, G. (2006). *Images of organization.* Thousand Oaks, CA: SAGE Publications.

Mulford, B., & Silins, H. (2003). Leadership for organisational learning and improved student outcomes—What do we know? *The Cambridge Journal of Education, 33*(2), 175–195.

Murphy, J. (1992). *The Landscape of Leadership Preparation.* Thousand Oaks, CA: Corwin Press.

National Association of Elementary School Principals. (2001). *Leading learning communities: Standards for what principals should know and be able to do.* Alexandria, VA: Author.

National Commission for Teaching and America's Future. (NCTAF). (1996). *What matters most: Teaching for America's future.* New York: Authors.

National Education Association. (2005, May). *It's About Time.* NEA Today. (http://www.highbeam.com/doc/1P3-829800071.html)

National Educational Commission on Time and Learning. (1994). *Prisoners of time.* Washington, DC: U.S. Government Printing Office.

National Staff Development Council. (2001). *Standards for staff development.* Oxford, OH: Authors.

Newmann, F. M. (1999). We can't get there from here: Critical issues in school reform. *Phi Delta Kappan, 80*(4), 288–294.

Newmann, F. M., & Wehlage, G. (1995). *Successful school restructuring.* Madison: Center on Organization and Restructuring of Schools, School of Education, University of Wisconsin.

No Child Left Behind Act of 2001, Pub. L. no. 107-110, 115 § 1425 (2002). Print.

Noguera, P. (2003). *City schools and the American dream.* New York: Teachers College Press.

Olivier, D. F. (2001). *Teacher personal and school culture characteristics in effective schools: Toward a model of a professional learning community.* Unpublished doctoral dissertation, Louisiana State University.

Olivier, D. F., Cowan, D. F., & Pankake, A. (April, 2000). *Professional learning communities: Cultural characteristics of supportive conditions and shared personal practice.* Paper presented at the annual meeting of the American Educational Research Association, New Orleans.

Olivier, D. F., & Hipp, K. K. (2006). Leadership capacity and collective efficacy: Interacting to sustain student learning in a professional learning community. *Journal of School Leadership, 16*(5), 505–519.

Olivier, D. F., Hipp, K. K., & Huffman, J. B. (2003). Professional learning community assessment. In J. B. Huffman & K. K. Hipp (Eds.), *Reculturing schools as professional learning communities* (pp. 70–74). Lanham, MD: The Scarecrow Press.

Olivier, D. F., Pankake, A., Hipp, K. K., Cowan, D. F., & Huffman, J. B. (April, 2005). *Longitudinal study of two institutionalized PLCs: Analyses of multiple variables within learning communities.* Paper presented at the annual meeting of the American Educational Research Association Conference, Montreal, Canada.

Ovando, M. N. (1994). *Effects of teachers' leadership on their teaching practices.* Paper presented at the annual conference of the University Council of Educational Administration, Philadelphia.

Pankake, A. M., & Moller, G. (2003). Overview of professional learning communities. In J. B. Huffman & K. K. Hipp (Eds.), *Reculturing schools as professional learning communities* (pp. 3–14). Lanham, MD: Scarecrow Education.

Patterson, K., Grenny, J., McMillan, R., & Switzler, A. (2002). *Crucial conversations: Tools for talking when stakes are high.* New York: McGraw-Hill.

Payne, R. K. (2005). *A framework for understanding poverty.* Highlands, TX: aha! Process, Inc.

Printy, S. M. (Winter, 2004). The professional impact of communities of practice. *UCEA Review, 46*(1), 20–23.

Protheroe, N. (2004). Professional learning communities. *Principal, 83*(5), 39–42. Retrieved July 22, 2009, from http://portal.ers.org/content/821/preview-naesp1251_professionallearningcommunitie.pdf.

Purnell, S., & Hill, P. (1992). *Time for reform.* Santa Monica, CA: Rand Corporation.

Reeves, D. B. (2006). *The learning leader: How to focus school improvement for better results.* Alexandria, VA: Association for Supervision and Curriculum Development.

Richardson, V., & Placier, P. (2001). Teacher change. In V. Richardson (Ed.), *Handbook of research on teaching* (4th ed., pp. 905–947). Washington, DC: American Educational Research Association.

Rosenholtz, S. J. (1989). *Teachers' workplace: The social organization of schools.* New York: Longman.

Sackney, L., Mitchell, C., & Walker, K. (April, 2005). *Building capacity for learning communities: A case study of fifteen successful schools.* Paper presented at the annual meeting of the American Educational Research Association, Montreal, Canada.

Schlechty, P. (1997). *Inventing better schools.* San Francisco: Jossey-Bass.

———. (2001). *Shaking up the schoolhouse: How to support and sustain educational innovation.* San Francisco: Jossey-Bass.

Schmoker, M. (2006). *Results now: How we can achieve unprecedented improvements in teaching and learning.* Alexandria, VA: Association for Supervision and Curriculum Development.

Schroth, G., Beaty, D., & Dunbar, B. (2003). *School scheduling strategies: New ways of finding time for students and staff.* Lancaster, PA: ProActive Publications.

Senge, P. M. (1990). *The fifth discipline: The art and practice of the learning organization.* New York: Currency/Doubleday.

———. (2000). *A fifth discipline resource: Schools that learn. A fifth discipline fieldbook for educators, parents, and everyone who cares about education.* New York: Currency Doubleday.

Senge, P., Cambron-McCabe, N., Lucas, T., Smith, B., Dutton, J., & Kleiner, A. (2000). *Schools that learn.* New York: Doubleday.

Senge, P., Kleiner, L., Roberts, C., Ross, R., & Smith, B. (1994). *The fifth discipline fieldbook.* New York: Doubleday.

Sergiovanni, T. J. (1994). *Building community in schools.* San Francisco: Jossey-Bass.

———. (1996). *Leadership for the schoolhouse: How is it different? Why is it important?* San Francisco: Jossey-Bass.

Sharratt, L., & Fullan, M. (2006). Accomplishing district-wide reform. *Journal of School Leadership, 16*(5), 583–595.

Short, P. M. (1994). Defining teacher empowerment. *Education, 114*(4), 488–492.

Silins, H., Mulford, B., & Zarins, S. (1999). *Leadership for organizational learning and student outcomes. The LOLSO Project: The first report of an Australian three year study of international significance.* Paper presented at the annual meeting of the American Educational Research Association, Montreal, Canada.

Snyder, K. J., Acker-Hocevar, M., & Snyder, K. M. (1996). Principals speak out on changing school work cultures. *Journal of Staff Development, 17*(1), 14–19.

Southwest Educational Development Laboratory. (2005). *Professional teaching and learning cycle: Introduction.* Austin, TX: Author.

Sparks, D. (1999). Real-life view: Here's what a true learning community looks like. *Journal of Staff Development, 20*(4), 53–57.

Spaulding, A. M. (1994). *The politics of the principal: Influencing teachers' school-based decision making.* Paper presented at the annual meeting of the American Educational Research Association, New Orleans.

Spelling, M. (2007). *Building on results: A blueprint for strengthening the No Child Left Behind Act.* Washington, DC: U.S. Department of Education.

Spillane, J. (2006). *Distributed leadership.* San Francisco: Jossey-Bass.

Spillane, J. P., & Diamond, J. B. (2007). *Distributed leadership in practice.* New York: Teachers College Press.

Stein, M. K. (1998). *High-performance learning communities District 2: Report on year one implementation of school learning communities.* High-performance training communities project. Washington, DC: ERIC (ERIC Document Reproduction Service No. ED429263).

Stoll L., McMahon, A., & Thomas, S. (2006). Identifying and leading effective learning communities. *Journal of School Leadership, 16*(5), 611–623.

Supovitz, J. A., & Christman, J. B. (November, 2003). Developing communities of instructional practice: Lessons from Cincinnati and Philadelphia. *CPRE Policy Briefs*, RB-39, 1–7.

Svec, V., Pourdavood, R. G., & Cowen, L. M. (1999). *Challenges of instructional leadership for reforming school.* Paper presented at the annual meeting of the American Educational Research Association, Montreal, Canada.

Tobia, E. (2007). The Professional Teaching and Learning Cycle: Implementing a standards-based approach to professional development. *SEDL Letter, 19*(1), 11–15.

Tschannen-Moran, M. (2004). *Trust matters: Leadership for successful schools.* San Francisco: Jossey-Bass.

U.S. Commission on Excellence in Education. (1983). *A nation at risk.* Washington, DC: U.S. Government Printing Office.

Valle, F. (2008). *Difficult but not impossible: Initiating comprehensive high school reform in a south Texas school district.* Unpublished dissertation, The University of Texas Pan American.

Walker, D. (2002). Constructivist leadership: Standards, equity, and learning—Weaving whole cloth from multiple strands. In D. Waler et al. (Eds.), *The Constructivist Leader* (2nd ed., pp. 1–33). New York: Teachers College Press.

Wallace Fellows project in cooperation with Cardinal Stritch University. (2007). *Urban school leadership: Managing magnitude, urgency and complexity.* Milwaukee, WI: Cardinal Stritch University.

———. (2008). *Urban school leadership: Success for the urban child, teacher and administrator.* Milwaukee, WI: Cardinal Stritch University.

Weber, P., & Hipp, K. K. (2009). Building leadership capacity in challenging schools. *International Journal of Urban Educational Leadership, 3*, 1–22. Retrieved from http://www.uc.edu/urbanleadership/current_issues.htm.

Wellman, B., & Lipton, L. (2004). *Data-driven dialogue: A facilitator's guide to collaborative inquiry.* Sherman, CT: Mira Via, LLC.

Wheatley, M. J. (2002). *Turning to one another: Simple conversations to restore hope to the future.* San Francisco: Berrett-Koehler.

Wiggins, G., & McTighe, J. (2006). Examining the teaching life. *Educational Leadership, 63*(6), 26–29.

Wignall, R. (1992). *Building a collaborative school culture: A case study of one woman in the principalship.* Paper presented at the European Conference on Educational Research, Enschede, The Netherlands.

Wilhelm, T. (2006). Professional learning communities for schools in sanctions. *Leadership, 36*(1), 32–33. Retrieved July 22, 2009, from http://www.thefree library.com/Professional+learning+communities+for+schools+in+sanctions:+ ...-a0152994010.

Wood, F. H., & Killian, J. (1998). Job-embedded learning makes the difference in school improvement. *Journal of Staff Development, 19*(1), 52–54.

Wood, F. H., & McQuarrie, F., Jr. (1999). On-the-job learning. *The Journal of Staff Development, 20*(3), 10–13.

Zempke (1999, September). Why organizations still aren't learning. *Training,* 40–49.

Zinn, L. F. (1997). *Supports and barriers to teacher leadership: Reports of teacher leaders.* Paper presented at the annual meeting of the American Educational Research Association, Chicago.

About the Contributors

Jesus "Chuey" Abrego, Ed.D. is an assistant professor in educational administration at the University of Texas at Brownsville and Texas Southmost College in Brownsville, Texas. He has served as an assistant principal and principal, state department of education, and university administrator. His research and teaching interests include professional development, professional learning communities, response-to-intervention, organizational change and leadership.

D'Ette Fly Cowan, Ed.D., is project director at SEDL, a private, nonprofit education research, development, and dissemination corporation, located in Austin, Texas. She is a contributing author to *Reculturing Schools as Professional Learning Communities* and *Learning Together, Leading Together*. She has served as an educational consultant, a school principal, and a reading teacher. Her research interests are educational leadership, organizational development, and systemic improvement.

Gayle Moller, Ph.D., is associate professor at Western Carolina University (Cullowhee, North Carolina) in the Department of Educational Leadership and Foundations. Her research interests are teacher leadership, professional development and professional learning communities. She is the coauthor of *Awakening the Sleeping Giant: Helping Teachers Develop as Leaders, 2nd Edition*, and *Lead with Me: A Principal's Guide to School Leadership*.

Dianne F. Olivier, Ph.D., is a retired educator with over thirty-three years of experience, twenty-six of those as a central office administrator. She currently trains for SREB and serves as an educational consultant in leadership, coaching, and school improvement. She has developed assessment measures relating to school culture, collective efficacy, and professional learning communities.

Anita M. Pankake, Ed.D., is a professor of educational leadership at the University of Texas Pan America in Edinburg, TX. She has served as a teacher, team leader, assistant principal and principal prior to working in higher education. She has served as a consultant on change and implementation in Wyoming, Kansas, Oklahoma and Texas. Her research and teaching interests include organizational change, leadership, gender issues and professional learning communities. She has authored, coauthored or coedited six books, more than twenty book chapters, and over seventy refereed and non-refereed articles. She is the coauthor of *Lead with Me: A Principal's Guide to Teacher Leadership* and is currently working with Elizabeth Murakami-Ramalho on an edited volume entitled, *Leadership for Social Justice: Encouraging the Development of Others.*

Linda C. Roundtree is a principal for the Milwaukee Public Schools in Milwaukee, Wisconsin. She is a contributing author to *Urban Leadership: Success for the Urban Child, Teacher and Administrator.* She has served as a district, state, and national presenter for both teachers and administrators. Linda has served as a school principal, Wallace Fellow, and a keynote to educational conferences and summits at all levels. She is highly recognized for sessions she co-presents with professors at Cardinal Stritch and National Louis-University on key topics such as "Empowering Women," new principal induction, professional learning communities, effective teaming practices, and teacher leadership. Her interests include becoming an effective superintendent of an urban district.

About the Editors

Kristine Kiefer Hipp, Ph.D., is an associate professor in leadership studies at Cardinal Stritch University in Milwaukee, Wisconsin. She consults widely facilitating organizational change in districts. Her research and teaching focus on leadership, developing cultures reflective of professional learning communities, collective efficacy, and personal transformation. She is coauthor of *Reculturing Schools as Professional Learning Communities*.

Jane Bumpers Huffman, Ed.D, is an associate professor in educational administration at the University of North Texas in Denton, Texas. Her research and teaching areas include change management, leadership, professional development, and professional learning communities. She is the coauthor of *Reculturing Schools as Professional Learning Communities*.